M000248191

Planning & Managing
EFFECTIVE
READING
INSTRUCTION
Across the Content Areas

A Strategic, Time-Saving Guide With Planning Sheets,
Model Lessons, and More to Help You Boost
Students' Comprehension and Learning

Deborah Corpus and Ann Giddings

📖SCHOLASTIC

New York • Toronto • London • Auckland • Sydney
Mexico City • New Delhi • Hong Kong • Buenos Aires

Dedication

In memory of our mothers, Bernadette Fuller and Margaret Hayner,

and

Debbie's husband, Jay

Acknowledgements

We thank the students, teachers, and administrators at Hattie B. Stokes School and Harney School in Lebanon, Indiana, and at Chapel Hill 7th and 8th Grade Center and Lynhurst 7th and 8th Grade Center in MSD of Wayne Township, Indianapolis, Indiana. They have welcomed us into their classrooms, observed our teaching, and offered their suggestions.

We thank our friends and colleagues at Butler University and in the Lebanon Community Schools, the MSD of Washington Township, Indianapolis, the Indiana Teachers of Writing, and the Indiana State Reading Association for their ongoing support and encouragement. Your suggestions and ideas have been so helpful. We appreciate the permission to use portions of an article by Debbie published in the *Indiana Reading Journal*, Summer 2007, as the basis for much of Chapter 2.

Our students in both undergraduate and graduate classes at Butler University and the teachers at Hattie B. Stokes School in Lebanon have graciously read portions of these chapters and offered ways to make the ideas work for beginning and practicing teachers.

We thank our students, past and present, who have taught us so much about teaching and learning.

Thanks, also, to Jeff Williams, literacy coach/consultant for Solon City Schools, Solon, Ohio, for so generously sharing his expertise.

Our editor, Sarah Glasscock, has been helpful and encouraging as we tackled this project. Thank you.

Most especially, we thank our families, who have supported us in this undertaking. Bob and Mary Grace Corpus cheerfully shared the kitchen table with this ongoing project and became even more self-sufficient as their mom focused on her writing. Larry Giddings offered a friendly reader's eye, thoughtful suggestions, and steady encouragement.

Scholastic grants teachers permission to photocopy the reproducible pages from this book for classroom use. No other part of this publication may be reproduced in whole or in part, or stored in a retrieval system, or transmitted in any form or by any means, electronic, mechanical, photocopying, recording, or otherwise, without permission of the publisher. For information regarding permission, write to Scholastic Professional Books, 555 Broadway, New York, NY 10012-3999.

Cover design by Jorge J. Namerow

Interior design by Melinda Belter

Interior photographs: Ann Giddings—pages 30, 116, and 133; Berry Wells—pages 79, 160–161

Editor: Sarah Glasscock

Copy Editor: David Klein

ISBN-13: 978-0-545-07480-3

ISBN-10: 0-545-07480-0

Copyright © 2010 Deborah Corpus and Ann Giddings

All rights reserved.

Printed in the U.S.A.

1 2 3 4 5 6 7 8 9 10   40   16 15 14 13 12 11 10

Contents

INTRODUCTION

In our professional lives, we see teachers become excited by all the new information about ways to teach reading, only to become discouraged by the increasing curricular demands across subject areas, the pressures of testing, and the overwhelming (and often contradictory) instructional programs their schools put in place. We hear legislators and business leaders broadcast their low regard for the profession by their demands for "teacher-proof" materials. We watch excitement turn to drudgery and resentment in both teachers and their students as their efforts became unfocused, and the main goal of our schools—raising happy, capable, literate adults—is forgotten. The work in this type of school setting is neither efficient nor effective.

We've used our experiences as teachers to guide our thinking in describing literacy instruction that is both efficient and effective across content areas. We've taken from own background experiences as teachers (over 30 years each), our training as Reading Recovery teachers, Ann's Reading Recovery Teacher Leader training and her work as a reading specialist at both the school and district levels in Lebanon, Indiana, and Debbie's experiences as a teacher and then central office K–12 curriculum coordinator in the Metropolitan School District of Washington Township in Indianapolis and her current work teaching Butler University education classes in public school settings.

In these pages, we've set out to share our insights to support thoughtful teachers in grades 3–8 who want to be efficient by teaching literacy strategies through the content areas. Echoing the words of the business management guru Peter Drucker, we know it's not enough to be efficient, simply getting the work done right. We also want to be effective in getting the right work done. To support teachers' desire to build effective lessons, we apply ideas and research found in *The Tipping Point* by Malcolm Gladwell so that all of us together can start a literacy epidemic. Our vision of that epidemic is a positive one: we want students who not only *can* read but who *do* read. We want a literacy epidemic that leaves avid, lifelong readers in its wake.

We aren't proposing new structures in this book. We rely on an apprenticeship model of teaching and learning, similar to that proposed by Regie Routman in *Reading Essentials* (2003), and we provide content-area-based literacy lessons in each aspect of that apprenticeship model: modeling, shared practice, guided practice, and independent practice. Our purpose is to make our reading instruction both more effective and efficient by deliberately teaching reading processes across content areas throughout the school day.

Below, we give a brief overview of the structure of our book. As you'll see, each chapter has a follow-up section that contains sample lessons and planning frames.

■ Chapter 1: We present an overview of both the apprenticeship model for literacy instruction and Gladwell's *The Tipping Point* as they can be applied to literacy.

- Chapters 2 and 3: These chapters and their follow-up materials look closely at the planning involved for efficient and effective instruction. Debbie focuses on modeling in Chapter 2 and shared practice in Chapter 3, and then follows each chapter with a section of specific examples and planning sheets for your own use.

- Chapter 4: Ann concentrates on individualizing instruction through guided reading based on the needs of the students you are teaching this year. A chart in the appendix spells out specific interventions for students who struggle with decoding, syntax, or comprehension issues.

- Chapter 5: We focus on setting up a system for independent reading. This chapter is your opportunity to help your students develop, in the words of Ann's mother, both roots and wings. You will see ways to guide your students in independent reading so that they have the knowledge, the roots, to be able to read independently. You will also guide them to develop joy in living a literate life, our version of wings.

A feature called "Your Turn" appears periodically in the book. The questions in this feature offer you time to think about connections to your own classroom, your own students. This is an invitation to stop, think, make notes, talk with other teachers, and simply make this book and these ideas your own.

Throughout the book, we are guided by the following four precepts for time management:

1. Time spent in planning saves time by allowing us to pace our lessons and make powerful, supportive connections among topics and lessons.

2. Time spent early in units and lessons in piquing students' interest and helping them make personal connections saves time in reteaching. It also avoids the possibility of students erecting emotional barriers to new learning.

3. Time spent in establishing cross-curricular connections saves time in building background knowledge as we move through the school year.

4. Time spent in planning effective lessons using information from Gladwell's *The Tipping Point* will save time in reteaching by making our lessons "stick," and can, in the long run, create a literacy epidemic.

Finally, as you read this book, we hope you will come to share our belief in using time efficiently and effectively by teaching reading through the content areas. If we are successful, we can all regain a sense of joy in our teaching while we share our love of reading with our students.

— Debbie and Ann

CHAPTER 1

The Big Picture: Planning a Year of Reading Instruction Across the Content Areas

I was in a classroom recently in which sustained silent reading was supposed to be going on. What I noticed was lots of fake reading, kids staring at the pages with their eyes fixed on a single point as everyone waited out the clock. I looked at the books in their hands. The books were new, but the titles were straight from the recommended reading list of 30 years ago. The principal had decreed that the only way to get kids to improve their reading test scores was to make them read grade-level material. He'd purchased classroom libraries of classics and expected students to read those books during their independent reading time. When I asked the teacher what she had done to "sell" the books to the students, she looked at me in surprise. She'd never read any of those books, she said, and she didn't want to waste her time reading them. If an adult didn't find those books enticing, why would anyone expect students to want to read them? (I won't even begin to deal with the assumption that the only way to get students to read on grade level for standardized tests is to force them to read books that are too difficult for them.)

In contrast to that classroom, let me tell you about another recent experience. I was asked to present at an after-school reading council meeting in a nearby city. I found myself in a second-year teacher's classroom. A handful of students had stayed after to help her straighten the room and put out snacks for the meeting. The sheer number of books in the classroom immediately struck me. Two large bookshelves were crammed with books, seemingly no two alike. When the students opened the doors of a cabinet, I saw that its shelves were filled with multiple copies of many titles, some of which I didn't recognize. I started asking some questions about those unfamiliar books, only to have the students tell me all about their author study of Jean Craighead George, hand me copies of their favorite mysteries, and simply overwhelm me with their enthusiasm for the books they had read. I left with at least six titles they made me promise to go home and read. I could tell there was no fake reading in that classroom. I could also tell that that second-year teacher knew something the first teacher did not. She knew how to introduce her students to a range of books and then help them share their discoveries and spread their passion for the books to others. A literacy epidemic was underway in her classroom.

— Debbie

What we are offering in this book is not the "teacher-proof" approach to planning and teaching found in the first teacher's classroom, where the principal mandated the methodology (sustained silent reading without teacher coaching), the amount of time (long silent stretches), and the books (classics such as *Call of the Wild, Return of the Native,* and *Wuthering Heights).* We are using a reflective teacher's approach to planning and teaching, as found in the second-year teacher's classroom. She used shared experiences and projects tailored to her own students, set aside time for reading throughout the day with invitations to take books home, and provided books of all types (including informational and literary classics) to feed her students' love of reading. She was engaged in a joyous cycle of planning and teaching as she worked with that specific group of students, tweaking and adapting her lessons to their interests and needs. The enthusiasm and knowledge generated by that young teacher and her students were palpable. Those students were becoming lifelong, avid readers.

Your Turn

Where do you put most of your time and efforts in planning lessons? In what ways are you effective and efficient?

Our conscious planning can make the difference. From a big picture perspective, what do we want our students to know and do? How can we plan our lessons so that their message "sticks"? How do we build a supportive context to nurture students' curiosity and drive to learn? If we are successful, our students will look back on their time with us as the beginning of their lifelong journey as readers. We will have started a literacy epidemic.

Planning to Teach Content and Reading

First things first. Before we begin to talk about lesson planning as a way to help our students grow and thrive as readers, we need to clarify what we mean by teaching reading *while* teaching content. Many people think teaching reading is simply teaching a long list of discrete skills. If reading is taught during content lessons, it is often taught as an add-on, an additional lesson that often shifts the students' attention away from the science, math, or social studies lesson. Instead of focusing on that discrete list of reading skills, we'll examine the processes all readers use, regardless of the type of materials they are reading. We want the reading instruction and support done during content-area time to be integral to the lessons taught, not a distraction. To be successful in teaching reading through the content areas, we believe the following elements are essential and nonnegotiable:

Content-Area Nonnegotiables

- Students must have access to *well-written texts* in all content areas.

- The focus for reading must be on *meaning and understanding* across the content areas.

Reading Nonnegotiables

- Readers actively think as they read: self-monitoring, cross-checking, searching for more information, self-correcting, listening to their internal voice for fluency of expression and phrasing.

- Readers employ various strategies as they read to help them understand, make connections, and remember what they have read.

- Readers are sensitive to the meanings of words in the context of what they are reading.

- Learning is socially constructed so that readers need opportunities to share their thinking.

- Choice of reading materials and ways to share engage readers so that they will want to have similar experiences.

We will explore these nonnegotiables further in the following sections.

Content-Area Nonnegotiables

Reading teachers are sometimes accused of teaching a contentless subject. Our main focus seems always on *process*, the how-to of reading. Depending on our curriculum and grade level, we teach students how to comprehend, how to read and remember new vocabulary, how to decode multisyllable words, and how to deal with complex syntax. Unfortunately, so often these reading processes are taught with insipid stories and bland encyclopedia-like articles. We avid readers would never willingly read such poorly written texts. Why then would we ever expect beginning or developing readers to read such texts, much less learn to love to read with them?

We also know that avid readers have a wide range of background knowledge developed story by story, book by book. Those avid readers make connections between what they already know and what they are learning as they read a social studies text or a science text. They are the ones who constantly interrupt us with discoveries of new connections: "This is just like when . . . ," or "This reminds me of . . . " They are our star pupils in social studies or health or science, not simply because they are good readers but because they are avid readers. They have developed a complex network of knowledge to which new knowledge is easily added.

Our first nonnegotiable is well-written texts. While it is true that teachers of reading do focus on the processes involved in effective reading, we are not limited to the texts supplied by publishers of reading programs. We have the broadest content possible: everything. Readers do not read simply to hear the words. We read about scientific discoveries, historical mysteries, the latest advances in health care, and the latest best seller because of the *content*. We are sponges, learning all that we can. So as teachers, our first loyalty must be to the content. We avid readers know it is the *content* of what we read that delights us, sustains us, and gives us refuge. We are charged by our curriculum with teaching specifics in history or science or literature or the arts, so we look for ways to teach reading processes through these content areas.

Our second nonnegotiable is that content is key. Each content area has its own specific list of content-based nonnegotiables. While we cannot address all the curricular objectives of every subject area in this slim volume, we will use examples of instruction from science, social studies, health, and literature. We firmly believe that to be efficient and effective in our teaching, we must teach not only the process of reading, but we must also simultaneously teach content. When students have finished a lesson with us, they must have added to their knowledge and understanding of the world in order for our lesson to have been truly effective.

Reading Nonnegotiables

It's easy to look at a social studies or science objective and know what facts students must understand, what terms they must be able to define, and what content we must teach. It's often more difficult to know what to teach when we teach reading processes in a content area. Too often, teachers think they are teaching reading only when they teach a story from a basal series or a literature anthology. Teaching a story, however, is teaching literature. It is not teaching a student how to read. Yes, our curriculum guides for the teaching of reading are filled with discrete skills that often focus on narratives, but what are the processes we teach when teaching reading across content areas? What is nonnegotiable when we teach reading?

✔ BASIC STRATEGIES

Regardless of reading level, there are basic strategies that all readers use. These are identified and explained more fully by Marie Clay, the New Zealand-born developmental psychologist and educator who developed Reading Recovery (Clay, 1993b), but here is an overview of what readers are constantly and simultaneously doing:

- **Self-monitoring:** Readers constantly ask themselves: "Does this make sense?" "Does this sound like English?" "Does this look right?"

- **Cross-checking:** Readers constantly monitor to check that what they read both makes sense and matches up with the letters on the page, that the structure of the sentence as read sounds possible in English, and that the structure of the word as read matches the letter cues on the page. (If, for example, a reader reads *house* for *home*, *house* means basically the same thing as *home* and would both make sense and fit syntactically in the sentence. It would not match all the letters on the page. A reader who is cross-checking would also expect to see the letter *s* toward the end of the word. If the reader didn't see that letter, then he or she would realize that something was wrong.)

- **Searching for more information:** If in self-monitoring or cross-checking the reader discovers there is a problem, he or she has ways to look for more information. The reader may look more closely at the letters of the word for phonic cues or reread the sentence for syntactic cues. He or she may reread or read ahead to try to figure out what is happening. The reader may ask someone or look up information for more clues to meaning issues.

- **Self-correcting:** After noticing a problem, a reader chooses when and how to self-correct. In the example above, it would be inefficient for a reader who mistakes *house* for *home* to go back to self-correct that error. All readers make mistakes as they read. (Tape yourself reading an unfamiliar article from *Scientific American* if you doubt this.) We operate at between 95% and 99% accuracy in most of our daily reading. We don't bother to self-correct unless we realize that something does not make sense or sound like English.

- **Fluency:** To read fluently and expressively so the text makes sense, a reader reads most words automatically in meaningful phrases, paces the reading according to the demands of the text's content and style (e.g., speeding up in exciting parts of a narrative, slowing down in thought-provoking or content-dense material), takes words apart while reading when decoding to look for familiar "chunks," and provides every word with at least a temporary pronunciation if the word is not in his or her speaking vocabulary.

✔ COMPREHENSION STRATEGIES

While current parlance lists comprehension as only one of the "big five" (Phonemic Awareness, Phonics, Comprehension, Vocabulary, and Fluency) to be addressed through No Child Left Behind legislation (Routman, 2003), its place in that list is deceptive. If we read without comprehension, we are not really reading; we are merely word calling. From children's very first contact with print through the rest of their lives, they must understand what they read. No adult reads the newspaper just to read the words correctly. While we may read poetry because we enjoy the sounds of the words, we also read it for the images and meaning that it gives us. Arthur Hyde, Steven Zemelman, and Harvey Daniels (2005) have framed the varying lists of comprehension strategies for teachers of all subject matters. Readers across content areas must visualize, make connections, ask questions, make inferences, evaluate information, analyze, recall, and self-monitor.

As we teach reading, especially in grades 3–8, we focus on those thinking strategies in all forms of content that students read.

✔ WORD STUDY

One gift a teacher gives his or her students is a sensitivity to and joy in the language. Why would we use *engaged* rather than *involved*? Where did the phrase "as easy as pie" originate? What is the specialized terminology that allows a mathematician to speak to other mathematicians or a musician to speak to other musicians? Why don't we change the spelling of a base word when its pronunciation changes, e.g., *medical* to *medicine*? How do words or phrases, such as *like* and *you know*, suddenly become common across the country? How do we give new words a temporary pronunciation as we read? How do we figure out their meaning or find out how others pronounce them? Part of our literacy instruction across content areas must focus on vocabulary and word use.

✔ SHARING

Harvey Daniels was the keynote speaker at the NCTE Middle Mosaic in 2006. In his presentation, Daniels outlined four practices that made a difference in the reading achievement of a school in which he worked:

1. Individualized, teacher-supported classroom libraries reflecting the teacher's interest and content-area specialty and planned time for sustained reading

2. A focus on vocabulary through content-area-specific word walls

3. Consistent use of turn-and-talk, written conversations, or other similar instructional methods for students to stop and interact to discuss what they were learning throughout lessons

4. Use of graphic organizers by students and teachers to visualize information and the relationships among ideas and to communicate those ideas visually to others

As I (Debbie) listened, I was struck by the common theme in all of these practices:

sharing. Teachers and students use language and visual representations to share their thinking about what they are learning. Russian psychologist Lev Vygotsky's theories (1962) clearly outline how a teacher's (or more learned other's) language can mediate and advance children's learning within their "zone of proximal development" (ZPD). (Also see pages 14–15 for more on ZPD.) In each of the four practices that Harvey Daniels outlined, the use of oral or visual language to mediate children's experience is clear. A nonnegotiable for us has to be the use of practices that encourage and support the sharing of emerging understandings in oral, written, and graphic forms.

✔ CHOICE

Regie Routman in *Reading Essentials* and Stephen Krashen in *The Power of Reading* (1993) make ironclad arguments that students respond best when given choices in their reading. We know that from personal experience as well. Ask college students about their high school reading, and they'll complain bitterly about the books they were required to read. (They'll also share many strategies for not reading and looking as though they were.) When a school faculty is told that everyone must read a particular professional development book, scowls and muttering fill the room.

It's human nature to resist. None of us wants to be forced or required to do something that takes time and thought. Reading takes both. Reading is a commitment, both emotionally and intellectually. In order for us to honor that commitment, we need to be able to choose the text to read. Our choices are based on our past experiences with authors and genres as well as our current needs. We may be on an author binge, reading everything by a particular author. We may be on a topic binge, reading everything about a subject that interests us. Sometimes these binges last a short time; sometimes they last a lifetime. Those of us of a certain age remember reading every Nancy Drew, Cherry Ames, or Trixie Beldon book we could find. Now, as adults, we may devour novels by Nicholas Sparks, John Grisham, Jane Austen, or Anne Rice. We may have ten different biographies of Theodore Roosevelt, shelves of various gardening books for shady areas, parenting advice collections, or financial advice tomes. We may have stacks of magazines with advice for decorating our houses, a pile of current news magazines, how-to books for our favorite sport or hobby, or books that make us laugh. We may download books to listen to as we exercise or drive. We make the emotional and intellectual commitment to read based on our interests and past experiences.

To help our students go on their own book binges, we first have to have a range of genres: collections of comic strips, joke books, mysteries, how-to books, nonfiction, biographies, picture-filled books, and almanacs. Wander through a well-run children's bookstore or library and note the range of attractive materials available for children. There are hundreds of publishers, so the books all have a different look to them. They come in many sizes and layouts. The collections do not look boring. A similar range of genres is available in each content area. We do not want our subject-area collections to look boring.

> ## *Your Turn*
> Do our nonnegotiables match yours? In what ways? If you had to teach on the proverbial desert island with no published curriculum or textbook to follow, what would you include to be sure your students were successful readers and learners?

Second, we have to have a range of levels available to all readers. As adult readers, we vary the level of difficulty of our own reading from serious professional books to light reading in *People* magazine. If we looked at the ratio of difficult reading we do to light reading, most of us would discover that we seldom read more than one difficult book or article out of every ten we read. We have to allow students the same flexibility. Encourage them to read widely, yes, but allow them to build the knowledge of structure and content that comes from going on author binges or topic binges. Encourage the light reading that builds fluency and automaticity.

Third, we have to introduce students to new possibilities through our read-alouds and our conversations about books. We also must recruit students to introduce new books and genres to each other through the systems of sharing that we put in place.

Choice keeps reading from becoming boring.

An Apprenticeship Into Reading

It's not enough to identify our nonnegotiables. We also have to ask ourselves what the best way to teach a process or skill is, and our answer comes from centuries of teaching people as individuals. The apprenticeship model of teaching and learning is based on the age-old concept that novices who are learning a craft or skill can be taught and guided by one who is both expert in this craft or skill *and* who understands how to lead the novice toward skillfulness. Many apprenticeship frameworks have been suggested, but perhaps the most aptly named is Regie Routman's Optimal Learning Model (Routman, 2003). Briefly stated, Routman plans for a gradual release of responsibility from teacher to student through defined instructional structures: demonstration, shared practice, guided practice, independent practice.

In this model, apprentices watch clear demonstrations of the whole process while they are carefully taught how to do some aspect of the process starting with the easiest of tasks. In the next step, the apprentice receives more responsibility along with more guidance, moving from the stage of helping the master do a task to actually doing the task under the master's watchful eye. Finally, the apprentice works independently using the skill or process learned but repeats the cycle of observation through guided practice, working independently on each new skill or process introduced.

Just so, our students who are developing readers are our apprentices. We demonstrate the act of reading so our students understand why they are learning individual strategies. We model, we guide their practice, and we supervise their independent use of these strategies. We also decide which skill or strategy they need next and repeat that teaching and learning cycle. Just as the master craftsperson would not expect a new apprentice to become instantly independent after one demonstration, neither would a reading teacher simply demonstrate a skill or strategy and then expect students to be able to use it independently in a range of materials and reading levels. We teachers of reading guide students toward proficiency through modeling, guiding, and overseeing our apprentices, and we support students as they test their fledgling strategies in increasingly more difficult or varied materials.

Apprenticeship Model Chart

MODELING	SHARED PRACTICE	GUIDED PRACTICE	INDEPENDENT PRACTICE
Teacher doing; Students watching	Teacher doing; Students helping	Students doing; Teacher helping	Students doing; Teacher watching

Modeling

In the first stage of the apprenticeship model, the teacher models the target reading skill or strategy for students so they can observe how proficient reading sounds and how a proficient reader uses that skill or process. Teachers can effectively model a reading behavior or process during a read-aloud framed as interactive reading.

Here's how Ann introduced a group of fourth-grade students to the Newbridge Discovery Links book *Nature Did it First* by Susan Ring. This book explores the similarities between nature and technology and describes how scientists get their ideas from the world of nature. As Ann previewed the book, she noticed that some of the chapters had a sidebar about a scientist or an inventor that connected with the description of the similarity between science and nature. She wanted students to understand the purpose of a sidebar and how it could be used to understand the content of the text, so she read aloud a section, "Lessons From a Spider," sharing out loud the questions that came to her mind: *Do engineers actually use the patterns of lines and spaces found in spider webs to design bridges? How could scientists re-create the stretchiness and strength of spiders' silk?* Then, displaying an overhead transparency of the sidebar titled "What Clues Do Spiders Hold?" at the end of the section, Ann read about Dr. Anne Moore, a biology professor who is actually researching spiders' silk. She asked the students to turn to a partner and talk about how knowing about Dr. Moore's research would help her to begin to answer the questions she had posed while reading the chapter. Ann explained that authors use sidebars to help readers understand their message as well as to pique interest in the subject.

Shared Practice

In the second stage of the apprenticeship model, shared practice, the teacher invites students to participate in the targeted behavior or thinking. This can happen during shared reading or guided reading, when students take on increasingly greater responsibility for engaging in the targeted behavior while the teacher gradually decreases his or her role.

Here's how Ann helped one group of fourth graders who needed greater support in reading the remainder of *Nature Did it First*. She met with this group to continue reading the text as a shared book. Each student had a copy of the book and followed along as Ann read a chapter and the sidebar for it. Together, Ann and the group members discussed the content of the chapter and sidebar, highlighting how the information in the sidebar expanded students' understanding of the content of the chapter. Ann was still doing the reading and thinking work, but the students were helping her, actively testing their understanding of the process against what they saw her, their teacher, doing.

Guided Practice

In the third stage of the model, the students do the work while the teacher is close at hand to notice when they are using the targeted strategy and to prompt when necessary to help those who have run into difficulty.

When Ann worked with the fourth graders, she had a group of six gather around her. She paired the students and asked them for their plan for reading the next section in *Nature Did it First*. She affirmed plans that included reading the sidebars and then prompted students to remember to make connections between the main message of the text and the example given in the sidebars. All the partners read together. One pair read silently. The other two pairs took turns reading quietly to each other. Each set of partners discussed the text together before Ann led the discussion. When everyone reached the end of the section, Ann asked individuals to retell what the text said. When a student made a connection between the information in the text and the example in the sidebar, Ann noticed and named the strategy for the group. She helped the group members recognize that they had learned both content (the science involved) and used a reading strategy (making connections).

Independent Practice

In the fourth stage of the apprenticeship model, students have internalized the new skill or strategy and can independently practice using what they have learned as they read on their own. An apprentice at this stage would be engaging in the craft with some unobtrusive supervision by the master. Similarly, a teacher still checks in with the student at this stage of learning, perhaps during an individual reading conference, but generally the student can apply what has been learned to new texts, first at an easy level and eventually at more challenging levels. At this stage, the master craftsperson or teacher must decide what skill or strategy this apprentice needs to learn next. The cycle repeats as the apprentice, the student, is introduced to new or more complex tasks.

In Ann's lesson, the *Nature Did it First* text was at an appropriate reading level for a different group of students to read mostly on their own with some guidance and scaffolding from her. For this group, Ann introduced the next chapter of *Nature Did it First* and asked students to continue reading it on their own. She asked these students to jot down in their reading notebooks any questions they had while reading the text and to put a sticky note next to one or two sentences in the sidebar that interested them. Ann checked with individuals, using prompting questions to help them clarify their thinking.

The Apprenticeship Model and the Zone of Proximal Development

Again, these four stages of teaching and learning are encompassed in Vygotsky's *Zone of Proximal Development* (1962). This zone (ZPD) refers to the area of teacher-student interaction defined on one end by what the student can do without assistance through the middle of the zone signifying what the student can do only with the help and support of the teacher and finally bounded at the end of the zone by what the student cannot do, even with teacher assistance.

Students can certainly do more with a teacher's support than they can do without it. A teacher who knows what his or her students can and cannot do as readers is able to design instruction that pushes the edge of students' learning, allowing them to engage in the targeted behavior and thinking. As students practice a new skill or strategy with teacher support and guidance, they begin to take control and develop mastery of that new learning.

To make this process effective and efficient, the teacher must adjust his or her support to appropriately meet the needs of students. Too much teacher support encourages dependence on the teacher, while too little support causes frustration. It's a bit of a balancing act for teachers to provide just enough support to allow students to successfully engage in the behavior or strategy without preempting the opportunity for them to learn and develop control. Think about teaching a child to tie his or her shoes. If a parent always names each step of the process before allowing the child to proceed with the next step, the child becomes overly dependent on the specific step-by-step coaching. If, on the other hand, the parent responds to a request for help with, "I've told you that before. Figure it out," the child may either be stymied or may try a way that is incorrect. A thoughtful teacher knows how much support is needed at a particular time for a particular student.

The teacher/student interaction within the ZPD extends what the student can do without help and shifts the area of learning toward more challenging skills and strategies. That successful interaction also fosters a student's confidence and willingness to keep trying and learning. The apprentice can see himself or herself as a craftsperson some day. (For more on ZPD, see Chapter 4, pages 91–96.)

Timely Planning

Debbie remembers with embarrassment the year that she and her students were so caught up in a literature theme of "mysteries" that they spent the whole first semester on that theme and had to cram all the required literature works in eighth grade into the second semester. She had not planned ahead by mapping out a better schedule for themes and required works through the year.

She also remembers blithely telling seventh-grade students the first week in the grade level (for both the students and her) to go home and read the first story in the literature book, the short story "The Pacing Goose," excerpted from Jessamyn West's *Friendly Persuasion* (1945), for discussion on Tuesday. That Tuesday morning, two students had dutifully read the story. The remaining 24 students sat defensively at their desks calling it "stupid" and "dumb" and swearing they'd never read anything out of that "boring" literature book again. Debbie learned the hard way three of the four precepts of time management we set out in the introduction and that guide us throughout this book:

1. Time spent in planning saves time by allowing us to pace our lessons and make powerful, supportive connections among topics and lessons.

2. Time spent early in units and lessons in piquing students' interest and helping them make personal connections saves time in reteaching. It also avoids the possibility of students erecting emotional barriers to new learning.

3. Time spent in establishing cross-curricular connections saves time in building background knowledge as we move through the school year.

Timely planning requires us to do big-picture planning so we know how our academic year will flow. It also requires us to do the nitty-gritty planning to make sure our individual lessons are effective.

Creating a Literacy Epidemic

What makes a unit or an individual lesson effective? Why do some lessons catch students' imagination and enthusiasm, while others seem to drag? A few years ago, we read Malcolm Gladwell's *The Tipping Point: How Little Things Can Make a Big Difference* (Gladwell, 2002), an influential and popular book that started us thinking. The fads outlined in the book, from the hula-hoop to the wearing of Docker shoes, didn't happen gradually. They swept the nation, seemingly overnight. Gladwell likens these fads to an epidemic with its three characteristics:

> *"One, contagiousness; two, the fact that little causes can have big effects; and three, that change happens not gradually but at one dramatic moment. . . . The name given to that one dramatic moment in an epidemic when everything can change all at once is the Tipping Point."* (Gladwell, 2002, p. 9)

We immediately began making parallels to our experiences in schools. Why do some fads seem to sweep through education? Why are we always reminded of the analogy of a pendulum swinging as we move from fad to fad? Can this idea of a tipping point help explain the rush to embrace big ideas: cooperative learning, whole language, leveling books, writing workshop? Does it explain the overnight popularity of commercial programs and tests, including 4 Blocks, the Shurley method, and DIBELS?

Perhaps each of these ideas was contagious because it promised great gains for what appeared to be common sense. Teaching students to work together, read real books, and write like real authors makes intuitive sense to people who are readers and writers. The wild success of other programs rests on even more seductive promises: They will save us time in planning, and they'll save us time in the school day—all while being easy to use.

We have to look at each new program and idea and ask ourselves the following questions: Who is offering it? What does it promise us? What contextual factors will make or break this program? How will we know if it does what was promised without unintended, negative side effects?

Let's look at some problem-solving solutions that have swept our schools in the last decades, and their outcomes:

- Who wouldn't see value in simplifying our busy day by organizing blocks of uninterrupted time? Highly regarded teachers and researchers, from Pat Cunningham and Richard Allington, authors of *Classrooms That Work* (2007) to Robert Slavins, chairman of the Success for All Foundation, responded to the frustration of days filled with pullouts, assemblies, announcements, and specials. These researchers offer uninterrupted blocks of time filled with specific literacy activities based on their differing (and at times contradictory) beliefs about reading instruction. The unintended consequence, though, was implementation at the school level that focused on time, not on instruction. We have not seen the promised improvement in student learning, but we have seen teachers frustrated by teaching to the clock. In one school in which Debbie worked, she counted 10 to 12 minutes of every hour spent walking kids in straight lines through the hallway from one tracked reading group, tutoring session, or reading lesson to another. Additionally, because so many teachers were responsible for struggling readers, no one was truly responsible.

- If we lack professional knowledge in an area (e.g., teaching grammar or writing), why not use a scripted program of music and chant to engage children? The Shurley Method capitalizes on the love of music and rhyme that we all experienced in the primary grades. The assumption, of course, is that students who can chant the definition of a particular part of speech will be able to use that understanding on standardized tests or in their writing. But the unintended consequence is that many students can sing the rhymes and chant the definitions but still cannot write well.

Your Turn

What educational fads have you experienced as a student or as a teacher?

Who advocated the idea? A guru? Legislators? A professional organization?

What made the idea attractive or sticky? What problem did it purport to solve with ease?

What was the social or educational situation that made the idea quick to spread?

In what ways was the idea or program effective in doing what was promised? Were there unintended consequences?

- If we need hard data, why not use a stopwatch and a one-minute sampling to check for reading fluency? The research seems clear: Students who read fluently are more apt to read with comprehension. Why waste time testing comprehension when we can simply measure reading speed and get data for mandated Reading First testing? The data seems clear, even while teachers and parents question the use of class time spent racing through lists of nonsense words instead of reading real books. We see the unintended consequence in schools where the focus is not on reading continuous text for meaning but on increasing the number of isolated words students can read in a minute through mindless drills.

All these ideas have been contagious. In many cases, though, they have been implemented in simplistic ways by following the script or teacher's manual. Most of them can be traced to seemingly small, easy changes, yet they have resulted in major, often unintended, negative effects on our practice. Gladwell gives us some ideas about what caused these ideas and programs to "tip" so they swept the country:

> There is more than one way to tip an epidemic, in other words. Epidemics are a function of the people who transmit infectious agents, the infectious agent itself, and the environment in which the infectious agent is operating. And when an epidemic tips, when it is jolted out of equilibrium, it tips because something has happened, some change has occurred in one (or two or three) of those areas. These agents of change I call the Law of the Few, the Stickiness Factor, and the Power of Context. (Gladwell, 2002, p.11)

Finding the Tipping Point in Literacy Instruction

As Gladwell points out, an epidemic has three contributing factors: (1) the Law of the Few: the power of connectors, mavens, and salespeople, (2) the Stickiness Factor: the message and how to make it memorable, and (3) the Power of Context: the specific, in-the-moment environment. In the next sections, we'll talk about how these factors apply to finding the tipping point in our literacy instruction.

✔ THE LAW OF THE FEW: THE POWER OF CONNECTORS, MAVENS, AND SALESPEOPLE

As teachers, we are the connectors, mavens, and salespeople. You can probably immediately think of how the teachers you know fit into these categories. They are easy to identify: Each parent wants her third grader in Miss Smith's class because her students always come home excited about the planned activities that bring social studies and science alive for them. No new reading program is accepted in the building without Mrs. Stout's approval because she simply is *the* authority. The eighth graders willingly work nights and weekends on any project assigned by the charismatic Mr. Minichello. Contagiousness in an epidemic is a factor of the messenger. (Gladwell, 2002, p. 233)

✔ THE STICKINESS FACTOR: THE MESSAGE AND HOW TO MAKE IT MEMORABLE

Making a message "sticky" or memorable means making it both practical and personal. In *The Tipping Point*, Gladwell explores the lessons learned from the television show *Sesame Street*: Children pay attention if the message makes sense; they look away if it is nonsense. He looks at the research from *Sesame Street* on repetition within the episodes, showing that repetition works if children are learning something with each repetition. He examines the research from another television show, *Blue's Clues*, and concludes that the problem has to be complex enough to engage interest but easy enough for early success. We were immediately reminded of Michael Smith and Jeff Wilhelm's research (2006) on boys' learning and especially their attraction to video games. The games are engaging, the boys learn something during each encounter, and the level of challenge changes with the boys' increasing aptitude. Those video game "lessons" are sticky. Stickiness is a factor of the message. Throughout Gladwell's work in *The Tipping Point* and Smith and Wilhelm's work with adolescents, we are reminded of the importance of joy. The message is stickier if there is in-the-moment enjoyment of the activity.

✔ THE POWER OF CONTEXT: THE SPECIFIC, IN-THE-MOMENT ENVIRONMENT

The power of context doesn't refer to a generalized environment but to the specific, in-the-moment environment. We think of the movie *Freedom Writers* and the power of the new books in that urban classroom to entice students and make them feel important for the first time in their academic lives. We think of Brenda Power's plea on the Choice Literacy Web site (2008) to clean out the clutter and bring some organization to our classrooms. Our students need the sense of order, peace, and control in order to feel they can get work accomplished. We are reminded of schools in Indiana following Barbara Pedersen's C.L.A.S.S. model (Connected *Learning* Assures *Successful Students*), in which classrooms are transformed into comfortable and inviting home-like areas with small table lamps, area rugs, and ruffled valences above the windows. Students feel welcome in those classrooms. We also think about negative factors in the environment: bullying, put-downs, lack of materials, and the way those factors undercut our efforts, keeping our message from sticking.

Planning a Literacy Epidemic

If we want our lessons to be effective, if we want to create an epidemic of literacy, we need to deliberately plan for the three factors of the epidemic: (1) the messenger, (2) the message, and (3) the context. We'll put aside, for the moment, our own effectiveness as the messenger—the person who is a connector, a maven, a salesperson—and the message itself—the content of what we are teaching. Instead, we'll first focus on the context and what to do to make sure that it is right so our message can spread. Just as it is easier to work to improve our family's health day-to-day if we start with a clean, organized home, it's also easier to work to improve our teaching day-to-day if the context in which we teach is organized.

Planning for Context

Our context for teaching includes our curriculum for what we are to teach (content and skills) and our general approach to teaching that curriculum. We can control our curriculum through our pacing and the interconnections we provide for students. We can control our own approach to the teaching of that curriculum, tweaking or adapting scripted lessons to fit our students' needs as apprentices.

✔ BIG-PICTURE PLANNING

To be efficient, we must teach the right curriculum effectively. In order to maintain our focus on the correct curriculum, we must do the big-picture planning first. Here are key questions we need to ask ourselves as we create an overarching plan for the year:

- What are the general topics of study for my students this year?
- What key process skills do students need to learn?
- How will what students learn in one subject area (e.g., inventors in science) connect with what they are learning in another subject area (e.g., biographies in literature)?

✔ MAPPING THE YEAR

Once we've looked at those big connections, those big building blocks of our school year, we have to see how they map onto the school year. To do that, here are some questions to ask ourselves:

- How do these building blocks from my big-picture planning map onto my teaching schedule, my own blocks of time?
- How do I sequence these blocks of time so that what students have learned in an earlier unit provides background for subsequent units?

Your Turn

Make a long timeline of your academic year. Plot in the school breaks, holidays, grading periods, etc. Now use sticky notes to write your big topics of study. Do not write "Science: Chapters 3–6." Write the topics. Look for connections and correlations across the topics. Then plot them along the timeline to see what fits where.

The first impulse of many teachers and grade-level teams is to simply block in time for each subject area and then plug in the academic standards for each subject, without regard for the interconnection between and among the standards. Successful teachers do not begin planning the year by simply plotting the state's academic standards or the testing objectives on a timeline. They think about the big picture of *how* those standards and objectives will be addressed through the content-area topics and projects; for example, using memoirs and biographies of famous Americans as reading material meets one of the reading standards. Those books can correlate with the history standards for our state in both fifth and eighth grades. Additional reading about those famous Americans can serve as the basis for the report writing required in those grade levels. The history textbook then becomes a secondary source of information for the history standards, rather than the only source. What is learned in one content area serves as background knowledge or reinforces what is learned in another.

THE APPRENTICESHIP MODEL IN ACTION

The next issue, of course, is planning for those big-picture topics. We must establish a context that will allow the literacy epidemic to spread. On page 15, we mentioned Debbie's attempt to introduce "The Pacing Goose" to her students. If only she had used an apprenticeship model that first week of seventh grade! Instead of assigning that short story for independent reading with the expectation of a stellar classroom discussion on Tuesday, she would have carefully planned the days devoted to the short story. Instead of seeing herself as "teaching the story," Debbie would have pinpointed *what* she was teaching that would provide background for everything else the rest of the school year. She would have modeled, provided shared practice and guided practice, and then observed while students worked independently. Debbie's thinking would have evolved something like this:

- I will identify my teaching points.

  Product: What is the main thing my students need to learn about reading literature that their experience with the story will provide? Perhaps my focus should be on using dialect and story details to understand a time period.

  Process: What is the main reading strategy my students will use or learn? My focus will need to be on visualizing while reading to understand the personalities involved.

- Next, I will look at connections: How does this story connect to what my students already know about Indiana history or that pre-Civil war time period or the Quaker religion? What do they already know about farm life or about the particular way of speaking found in this Quaker home? What will they understand about the human condition when they read about a man trapped by his own words into letting his wife raise a pet goose, an animal he hates? Will they understand why the husband would ask somebody else, an employee, to tamper with the eggs to keep them from hatching, rather than destroy the eggs himself? Will they understand the handyman's reluctance to destroy all the eggs and hurt the wife's feelings, a woman who has fed him and generally been "mighty kind" to him? Will they be able to predict how the woman would treat the sole gosling that hatches? I can use prediction riddles to introduce the characters, the story problem, and some key vocabulary.

- Then, I will model how to read dialect, perhaps using a readers' theater format for the dialogue as I move into shared practice. We can do some guided reading through partner work for the middle portion of the story, as the couple waits for the eggs to hatch. As independent practice, students can read the last part of the story silently or with partners during class as I work with a group of struggling readers to discover what happens when this pacifist Quaker woman takes her neighbors to court over a goose.

- Throughout it all, I will have ways to check on students' growing success in visualizing the story and handling dialect, while being alert for unintended consequences.

These structures of modeling, shared practice, guided practice, and independent practice are the ones we will be using in our planning framework throughout this book. A chapter will be devoted to each aspect of this planning framework so that you can plan effectively and not fall into the trap of quickly *assigning, assessing* under a cloud of failure, and then *reteaching* disengaged and disillusioned students.

Our view of context is not complete with a look at timelines and planning frames. We also have to focus on the social context within our classrooms. In *Reading Essentials,* Regie Routman highlights the necessity of bonding with our students. The work from the Developmental Studies Center focuses on classroom cultures to support children's academic, ethical, and social development. These works and our own experiences as teachers have taught us the importance of the social context within our classrooms. The routines and procedures we establish, embedded within a context of caring for our students as individuals, provide the culture so a literacy epidemic can occur. A charismatic, enthusiastic, caring teacher's lessons are memorable when students feel emotionally safe. The teacher sets the context for learning. He or she is also a powerful messenger for a literacy epidemic.

Planning To Be the Messenger: Bringing a Sense of Joy to the Cycle

If we want to start a literacy epidemic, we have to be both skilled teachers and avid readers. In the words of Gladwell's *The Tipping Point,* we need to be the maven, the connector, and the salesperson.

As a maven, we share our passion for reading. That means we need to nourish our own passion, carving out time even during the school year for personal reading and writing. We need to find and share resources with other teachers: the books too good to miss, the bookstore with the teacher discount, the column in our professional journal that points us to books we just have to share.

As a connector, we know how to find the right book at the right time for our students and our friends. We read *Book Crush* by Nancy Pearl and share the author's ideas with friends. We mark up our own copies of books. We keep a personal library of books, magazines, and journals to revisit and share. We bookmark Web sites that help us in our thinking, and we send those links to our colleagues. We organize our classrooms in simple, manageable ways so that the just-right books can be found easily. We share tips for management. We read ahead, knowing that there may not be time to do all the preparatory reading at the last minute. We participate in professional conferences and organizations because we are sponges for new information. Planning for teaching and for our role as both a maven and a connector needs to be part of the fabric of our day.

We also become salespeople, using the research on motivation and engagement by Michael Smith and Jeffrey Wilhelm (2006) to encourage a sense of "flow." We invite students with engaging tasks and challenges appropriate to their developmental levels, while supporting them with clear rules and feedback. We save time through cooperative learning routines and strategies. We celebrate children's successes and approximations. We save time and shape instruction through our assessments and record-keeping practices. We share our own enjoyment of books by planning instruction that is responsive to students' needs and interests.

Planning the Message: Making It Sticky

Finally, as the salespeople of reading, we plan to make our lessons memorable, or, using *The Tipping Point* terminology, we are sure the message is sticky. Look carefully at what we ask students to read. Would you want a steady diet of those materials? Are students reading only the textbooks, eating the same portions out of the same compartments of their metaphorical cafeteria tray? Are they consuming only literary fluff and nonsense, the equivalent of a fast-food diet? Are the reading materials old and unattractive? (One of Debbie's college students was working in a practicum setting in the same elementary school he had once attended. He picked up a tattered paperback book being used in a fourth-grade class and discovered his name written on the inside front cover from the long-ago day he'd been assigned that same book. We won't even begin to make the analogy to leftovers at this point.)

In addition to looking at our resources, we also need to look at how we sequence and deliver our lessons to make them memorable. In *The Tipping Point*, Gladwell gives us three ways to package a message to make it sticky:

1. Change the presentation to make it more practical and personal.

2. Use repetition strategically so the audience is actively involved with each repetition.

3. Encourage interaction through the message so the audience must do something. (Gladwell, 2002, p. 132)

As we plan for our literacy epidemic from our big picture to our daily plans, we have to consciously plan for our role as the messenger, our texts as the message, and our classroom and school as our context. Then we have to reflect. Gladwell points out, "Those who are successful at creating social epidemics do not just do what they think is right. They deliberately test their intuitions. . . . What must underline successful epidemics, in the end, is a bedrock belief that change is possible, that people can radically transform their behavior or beliefs in the face of the right kind of impetus." (Gladwell, 2002, p. 258)

To Sum it Up

We want the love of reading to be epidemic. If Gladwell is right, if our intuitions are right, we can set a literacy epidemic in motion in our classrooms. We can do that not by making huge, sweeping changes but by looking at the little things that can make a big difference. We can use our time effectively and efficiently as messengers. We can match students to sticky texts. We can tweak the environment to speed the message along.

Earlier in the chapter, we introduced three precepts that have guided our thinking:

1. Time spent in planning saves time by allowing us to pace our lessons and make powerful, supportive connections among topics and lessons.

2. Time spent early in units and lessons in piquing students' interest and helping them make personal connections saves time in reteaching. It also avoids the possibility of students erecting emotional barriers to new learning.

3. Time spent in establishing cross-curricular connections saves time in building background knowledge as we move through the school year.

Now, thanks to Malcolm Gladwell's work, we add a fourth precept:

4. Time spent in planning effective lessons using information from Gladwell's *The Tipping Point* will save time in reteaching by making our lessons "stick," and can, in the long run, create a literacy epidemic.

In the following chapters, we look at each aspect of the instructional continuum, from modeling through shared and guided practice to independent practice. You are invited to choose your own route through this book. Select the chapters that most fit your interests and needs right now. Browse the follow-up section after each chapter for sample lessons and planning frames, then go back to the chapters to read more about them as you have time. Mark up the book, note ideas in the margins, make connections to instructional methods that have worked for you, share what works for you with your teacher friends.

We invite you, the reader, to explore your own thinking, test your own intuitions. What is the right combination of messenger, message, and situation to create an epidemic of avid readers in your classroom? Our hope is that our work will help you move from a dread of planning to a cycle of planning that is joyful and engaging. Let the literacy epidemic begin!

Your Turn

1. Draft a brag sheet for yourself. What topics, subjects, books thrill you and make you a maven? A connector? A salesperson?
2. Write brag sheets for your colleagues. What are their areas of interest and expertise that complement your own?
3. When have you experienced the just-right combination of situation, teacher, and texts to become immersed in an instructional unit? What were the elements that made that unit so successful?

A Closer Look at Big-Picture Planning

As we plan, we must plan to work in a focused way to get the work done. We must test our intuitions to try different approaches to see which is most effective. We need to keep in mind the non-negotiables outlined in Chapter 1.

NONNEGOTIABLES:

Content-Area Nonnegotiables

- Readers need well-written texts.

- Content is key to deepening background knowledge and making cross-curricular connections.

Reading Nonnegotiables

- We teach these basic reading strategies throughout all subject areas:

  Self-monitoring

  Cross-checking

  Searching for more information (phonic, syntactic, semantic)

  Self-correcting

  Fluency (meaningfully phrased, fluent reading, paced according to the demands of the text's content and style)

- We focus on these comprehension strategies in all forms of content: visualizing, connecting, questioning, inferring, evaluating, analyzing, recalling, and self-monitoring.

- We conduct word study as we teach our content, not in isolated lessons.

- We incorporate different forms of writing and use graphic organizers to keep track of our thinking and share it with others.

- Students have a variety of texts to choose from, including, but not limited to, textbooks.

Planning for Units of Study and Inquiry

To work in a focused way, we need both big-picture planning (across the academic year) and short-term planning (at the unit level and lesson level). In the next sections, Debbie develops a plan for a multidisciplinary unit on inventors and inventions for grade 3 as an example.

Planning for the Year: A Sample

A few of the academic standards that third-grade teachers in Indiana must address during the academic year are shown on the next page. Teachers could "cover" the standards one-by-one, dragging themselves and their students through the year, or they could thoughtfully plan ways to focus their energies on the heart of these standards.

Selected Indiana Academic Standards for Grade 3:

Science Grade 3, Standard 1: Students, working collaboratively, carry out investigations. They question, observe, and make accurate measurements. Students increase their use of tools, record data in journals, and communicate results through chart, graph, written, and verbal forms.

Indiana Academic Standards, Science Grade 3, Standard 2: Students use a variety of skills and techniques when attempting to answer questions and solve problems. They describe their observations accurately and clearly, using numbers, words, and sketches, and are able to communicate their thinking to others.

Indiana Academic Standards, English/Language Arts Grade 3.2.6: Locate appropriate and significant information from the text, including problems and solutions.

Indiana Academic Standards, English/Language Arts 3.5.8: Write or deliver a research report that has been developed using a systematic research process (defines the topic, gathers information, determines credibility, reports findings) and that:

> Uses a variety of sources (books, technology, pictures, charts, tables of contents, diagrams) and documents sources (titles and authors).

> Organizes information by categorizing it into more than one category (such as living and nonliving, hot and cold) or includes information gained through observation.

Big-Picture Planning

Before we can plan our daily or weekly lessons, we have to know where we are heading and why. We need to do big-picture planning. We also need to identify the key topics we are required to teach in our grade level.

A word of caution is necessary here. Debbie found in her 12 years as curriculum coordinator that a number of topics were taught at a particular grade level, not because they were required but because that was the tradition. She found that simple machines, for example, were taught every year in kindergarten through grade 3 in a particular school because the teachers had taken the topics with them when they changed grade levels. They had the materials, they had the lessons, and they enjoyed teaching the topics, so they had simply continued to teach the unit, regardless of the grade level they were assigned. At one of the middle schools, Debbie discovered that the seventh-grade teachers did not have time to teach a required literature topic because they had always taught "the research paper" and parents expected it. The research paper, however, was not required in the curriculum until the following year. We need to distinguish between what we *must* teach and what we *want* to teach. If we have additional time in the curriculum, we should follow the students' interests, not tradition.

Part of big-picture planning includes identifying skills and processes that students need to learn in that particular grade level. Do students need to learn to use hydrometers and pipettes in science in order to study water density? If so, do they understand measuring liquids in milliliters? Do they understand how to write information in a table?

The third part of big-picture planning, then, is to look at our connections between and among content areas. How can we sequence our lessons so that each builds background knowledge for another?

✔ ASKING THE BIG QUESTIONS

Based on my grade-level curriculum, what is my destination, the basic message I'm delivering in this unit I'm planning? Using the Indiana Academic Standards listed above, I could summarize the main ideas I want students to learn in this way:

- *Scientists/inventors observe, take notes over time, make predictions, and test those hypotheses.*
- *Scientists/inventors often collaborate with others. They communicate their findings to others.*

Now I want to build in elements from *The Tipping Point* to make this unit of study memorable. How can I package my lessons to make the message sticky?

- How can I make this practical and personal?

- How can I use repetition and involve the students with each repetition?

- What will students be doing so they are actively interacting with the message?

✔ USING A FRAMEWORK

An easy way to do big-picture planning is to use a before/during/after frame, such as the Big-Picture Planning Chart on page 32. I use the chart to answer the following questions:

Before: How will I set this up to engage student interest?

During: What will I do to teach and then guide the students?

After: How will we follow up on this focused unit to bring a sense of closure, celebration, and an invitation for extensions to the learning?

Below, I show how I developed the Big-Picture Planning Chart for the third-grade interdisciplinary unit on inventors and inventions. The sample appears on the next page.

First Column: *I begin by thinking about how to set up the unit to engage my students and then write my ideas in the first column.*

Third Column: *Next, I plan an end goal for the unit, so I consider the following questions to help me fill in the third column:*

- *What culminating project or experience will engage students in using all that they have learned in this unit in a practical and personal way?*

- *How will I evaluate this project or experience? What is the preliminary rubric for evaluation?*

Second Column: *Now I want to think about what new information and skills students will need in order to successfully complete the culminating project or experience. The following questions guide me in filling in the second column:*

- *How will I model this process?*

- *How will I use shared practice?*

- *How will I use guided practice?*

- *How will I provide opportunities for independent practice?*

- *How can I tie these experiences back to the anchor text(s) and initiating experiences?*

- *When and how will I assess students' understanding throughout the unit so I can adjust my teaching?*

Big-Picture Planning Chart: Third-Grade Interdisciplinary Unit of Inventors and Inventions		
ANCHOR TEXT(S) AND/OR INITIATING EXPERIENCE:	ACTIVE TEACHING (CYCLING THROUGH MODELING, SHARED PRACTICE, GUIDED PRACTICE, INDEPENDENT PRACTICE WITH EACH NEW SKILL OR STRATEGY)	CULMINATING PROJECT OR EXPERIENCE AND KEY ELEMENTS OF RUBRIC FOR EVALUATION
Read aloud <u>So You Want to Be an Inventor.</u> Use graphic organizer on chart to keep track of inventor, problem to be solved, and invention. Have students "become" the inventors as I read. I'll hand them the invention or a picture of it as invention is mentioned and have them write their inventor's information on the chart.	<u>Modeling:</u> Connection to initiating experience: Assessment method: <u>Shared practice:</u> Connection to initiating experience: Assessment method: <u>Guided practice:</u> Connection to initiating experience: Assessment method: <u>Independent practice:</u> Connection to initiating experience: Assessment method: <u>Science</u> Intro with tangram problems Sink-it experiments and graphing Readings from textbook and science sources on buoyancy and density <u>Language arts:</u> Working in small groups with roles Skimming for specific information about inventors, inventions, and science principles	Groups of students will work together to "invent" a model raft to find a design that bears the most weight. They will share their inventions with the class. These inventions may be replicas of real inventions or original. The inventions must be based on science principles, not fantasy. Preliminary Rubric: 1. Identification and/or explanation of a problem 2. Evidence of attempts to solve the problem including notes over at least three trials 3. Ability to use simple scientific tools correctly 4. Ability to explain the physical properties involved including use of correct scientific terminology 5. Ability to collaborate positively with others

Sample Big-Picture Planning chart

✔ MAPPING THE YEAR

I think this unit of study will engage my students on many levels and address the standards. Now I have to turn this chart into a practical plan. I have to fit the unit into my lesson plan book so that it works with the school and grade-level calendar. The nitty-gritty detail level begins.

While I want to provide rich experiences so that learning is multilevel, I don't want to be so unfocused that my students walk away from the lessons wondering what they were supposed to have learned. To provide focus, I have to answer these questions:

- What are the one or two key teaching points for each day?

- How do I sequence the lessons so that my instruction builds and makes sense?

Here's the sequence of lessons for my third-grade interdisciplinary unit on inventors and inventions:

Sequence of Lessons: Third-Grade Interdisciplinary Unit of Inventors and Inventions

Day 1	Day 2	Day 3	Day 4	Day 5
Introduce anchor book and semantic feature map: Key ideas: inventors notice problems, make multiple attempts to solve them, and keep track of their thinking	Make connection to anchor book and key ideas of multiple attempts and keeping track of one's thinking as a scientist Model observing and taking notes on multiple attempts using tangrams • Provide shared practice and guided practice using tangrams • Model presentation to the class of my findings (Observation as assessment for teacher planning)	Make connection to anchor book: noticing a problem and keeping track of one's attempts to solve a problem: "Sink It" activities from Indiana Academic Standards Resources • Model making a prediction (Sink? Float?), charting it, doing the experiment, charting it, and making observations • Put students in groups of four. Assign roles that will rotate: Predictor, Scribe, Tester, Group leader. Provide shared practice by walking them through first four attempts. • Guided practice with next four items/rotations. • Independent practice next four items/rotations. (Observation and review of the group notes as assessment for teacher planning)	Remind students of experiment and use of notes. Model how to share outcomes. Have students practice sharing in their small groups. Have groups share for each item. Have student keep class chart of results and rationales. • Question the class: Based on your observations, what makes some things sink and some things float? Four minute quick write of hypotheses. (Observation and review of quick writes as assessment for teacher planning)	Give an overview of some of the hypotheses from the previous class. Show on a graphic organizer. Distribute graphic organizers, packets of information from various sources about sinking and floating, and textbook to groups. Model skimming to find information to answer our questions about why things sink or float. Chart answers on graphic organizer by resource. Have same groups work together to skim for information and chart it. Pairs of students within groups should buddy read an article, agree on information to chart, and chart it. Each pair should share information they found with other pair. Guided discussion: What did we discover? What questions do we still have? What are key terms scientists would use? Model: Writing a summary statement. Debrief group work: How did the groups work well together? How could they function better?

Sequence of Lessons: Third-Grade Interdisciplinary Unit of Inventors and Inventions

Day 6	Day 7	Day	Day	Day
The challenge: Based on what you've learned about sinking and floating and using items available in this classroom, construct a raft that will stay afloat with the most number of pennies on it. • Model experimenting with two rafts as pennies are put one-by-one on them. Chart your results. Summarize and make predictions for a better design. • Shared practice: groups of four, assign rotating roles: Penny-loader, Recorder, Summarizer, Group leader/Time Keeper. Pairs of students work together to build a raft. • Guided practice: Teacher as mentor; 20 minutes per building and testing rotation (Observation and notes as informal assessments to guide teaching) Assignment: Use what you know to help your group plan and build the most buoyant raft.	Raft building and testing. As a class, chart the results and the explanations. Focus on the scientific terms and basic understandings. (Teacher assessment using rubric) (Note: the understandings are important, not the winning.) • Debrief group collaboration. What went well? What could be improved? What steps will the group take?			

Sample Sequence of Lessons chart

To be practical, I also have to ask: How do I fit these lessons in my school calendar? I'm going to map out a one-hour afternoon block that combines language arts and science.

Monday–Friday Calendar: Third-Grade Interdisciplinary Unit of Inventors and Inventions				
Monday	**Tuesday**	**Wednesday**	**Thursday**	**Friday**
Read aloud anchor text	Tangrams	Half-day for teacher inservice	Sink It activity	Small group Sink It experiments
Skimming for specific information	Group challenge activity	All-class challenge activity	Catch-up day/ summary day	All-school convocation

WEEK 1 applies to the first data row and *WEEK 2* applies to the second data row.

Sample Monday–Friday Calendar

Flexibility in Daily Planning

This is truly big-picture planning. I don't have all the details worked out yet. A substitute couldn't come in and teach this unit from these preliminary plans. I do, however, have a basic idea that I can fit within my school calendar and grade-level calendar to teach and assess key required academic standards. I've done the initial work to make the message sticky and to put myself in the role of connector/maven/salesperson. I've planned for active engagement and problem-solving by students. While I'm teaching this unit, and afterward, I'll observe students' responses to see how to tweak the message or the delivery to make it stickier for this particular group of students. Because I'm working with an apprenticeship model in mind, I know I have to observe and assess my apprentices, my students, so I can determine when and how to start moving them from being dependent on me to gaining independence in this unit.

I may have to do more preparatory work on ways in which students cooperate with one another in the small groups so everyone feels safe to explore. I may have to change the challenge a bit so that competition doesn't overcome the message. I may have to find additional ways in which to support individual learners, either by the partners I choose for them or the materials I give them. I cannot script this unit to work in every classroom as is. I have to tailor it to the students in my classroom right now. Big-picture planning simply sets the course and the parameters for us.

As part of the modeling process, the teacher reads aloud.

✔ PACING THE LESSONS

Another consideration to make when you move to intermediate-level planning is to look at multiple subjects across this span of time. Think of how you're going to *pace* the activities. You don't want to schedule three different hands-on, messy activities for the same day. The amount of setup and cleanup will discourage you, and students will not be able to focus because of all the activity. If you are doing hands-on science after lunch, you may want to precede it by some quieter activities in subject areas that are not incorporated into the unit that day. Students might be doing shared reading in social studies and working on drafting and revising a story before lunch. On the other hand, you don't want a day filled with one writing task after another or one period of extended reading in one subject followed by another period of extended reading in another subject.

If you are teaching in a departmentalized setting, you really need to be aware of other teachers' big-picture planning. If all the eighth graders are immersed in the science fair for one teacher, you don't want to overwhelm them by scheduling a major essay contest integrating social studies research and English for the same time period. At the same time, students shouldn't be reading quietly during first-period English, reading in their social studies text during second period, taking a science test in the third period, reading yet again in fourth period art, and so on throughout a single day. If possible, dovetail themes and units across disciplines by grade level in a departmentalized setting and work with colleagues to be sure the pace of each day is varied for students.

Your Turn: An Invitation

Now it's your turn. Try integrating disciplines with reading instruction as you do big- picture planning for extended units. You can start with the academic-year calendar you mapped in Chapter 1 (see pages 19–20).

- Start with a content-specific theme or topic to focus your thinking. Complete the Content Areas and Academic Standards and/or Objectives form on page 33.

- Plot out the before/during/after ideas on the Big-Picture Planning Chart on page 32. Start with the initiating idea and then map out the culminating experiences. Next map out possible ways to teach and guide students between those two points.

- Estimate the number of days it will take you to teach the unit and the activities by chunking them by day on the Sequence of Lessons Schedule on page 34. Make multiple copies of the form for lessons longer than 5 days. You probably don't want to go beyond 15 days, for sanity's sake. Too much of a good thing can kill an idea, too!

- Finally, if you know when you want to teach the unit in a grading period, tentatively map in the days on the Monday–Friday Calendar on page 35. Check for interference from schoolwide or grade-level events. Think about what else you will be teaching on those days to make sure your pacing through the day will keep students engaged but not overwhelmed or underinvolved. Make sure the big- picture context is conducive to the message you're delivering.

The first test is this: When parents ask their child at the end of the day, "What did you learn today?" or "What did you do today?" the answer shouldn't be "nothing." If the message stuck, if you planned your class's trip through the school year, your enthusiasm as salesperson, mentor, and connector should have transferred to the students. They, in turn, should be able to share their enthusiasm and new learning with others.

The second test is this: At the end of the day, do you feel the satisfaction of having fostered independence so your students can and will use the skills and strategies independently? Have you created a literacy tipping point in our classroom?

Big-Picture Planning Chart:

ANCHOR TEXT(S) AND/OR INITIATING EXPERIENCE:	ACTIVE TEACHING (CYCLING THROUGH MODELING, SHARED PRACTICE, GUIDED PRACTICE, INDEPENDENT PRACTICE WITH EACH NEW SKILL OR STRATEGY)	CULMINATING PROJECT OR EXPERIENCE AND KEY ELEMENTS OF RUBRIC FOR EVALUATION

Content Areas and Academic Standards and/or Objectives

CONTENT AREA(S)/ MAJOR TOPIC	ACADEMIC STANDARDS ADN/OR OBJECTIVES

Sequence of Lessons:

DAY _____	DAY _____	DAY _____	DAY _____	DAY _____

Monday–Friday Calendar:

	MONDAY	TUESDAY	WEDNESDAY	THURSDAY	FRIDAY
WEEK 1					
WEEK 2					

CHAPTER 2

Planning for Effective Read-Alouds

It is the first day of my class for college juniors who want to become teachers. Some of them are avid readers, but many have not read anything for pleasure since middle school. Many come with the typical misconception that teaching reading is simply teaching decoding. Before talking to them about all that is involved in reading across content areas, I have the students experience the complexities through a shared read-aloud.

I put Allen Say's *Grandfather's Journey* on the document camera so everyone can see the picture on the cover. "What do you notice?" I ask, and then I have partners work together to notice details in the picture and predict why they might be significant.

"He looks Chinese or Japanese."

"His clothes are old-fashioned. Look at that hat and those gloves. Look at the rounded collar."

"His clothes look too big. Could it be that they didn't have any European sizes small enough for him?"

"He's on a ship. Maybe this journey takes place before airplanes. Yeah. The old-fashioned clothes make sense with that idea."

As I begin reading, I ask student to notice details and jot down questions that come to their minds. They are struck by the contrast between the first picture, a formal portrait of the main character looking very confident and strong in traditional Japanese garb, and the second picture, the same as the one of the front cover, where the man looks almost ludicrous.

The students nod in recognition at the pictures of the various places the character visits. I see some pencils moving, jotting down questions. "What parts of the country did he visit?" "What did he use for money?" They smile when they see the Japanese man in his too-large clothing, standing in front of a western town's barbershop flanked by a number of men. Allen Say writes, "He met many people along the way. He shook hands with black men and white men, with yellow men and red men." I see some pencils move again. "No prejudice?" some have written.

The story continues with the young man returning to Japan to marry his childhood sweetheart and then coming back to America to start his family. More penciled questions: "Did he love his wife or was it honor that sent him back to Japan?" "Did he have to go to Japan to find a wife? Would he have been allowed to marry anyone in this country who wasn't Japanese?"

The picture of his dark-haired daughter with her blond-haired, blue-eyed doll starts more pencils moving. "What would it have been like to grow up Japanese in California then?"

When I come to the point in the story, in which the father, homesick for Japan, moves his family back there after his daughter graduates from high school, the pencils really fly. These 20-year-olds have all sorts of questions about the daughter's reactions to being moved to a country that is foreign to her.

The story continues. The grandfather is happy in Japan but misses California. He tells his grandson all about the mountains and rivers there and even raises warblers and silvereyes to remind himself of the birds in the western United States.

His plans to make a trip to the United States are dashed by the onset of war. The students jot questions: "WWII?" "Atomic bomb?" "Does Grandfather hate the US now?"

Then I read the last pages of the book:

"And when I was nearly grown, I left home and went to see California for myself.

After a time, I came to love the land my grandfather had loved, and I stayed on and on until I had a daughter of my own.

But I also miss the mountains and rivers of my childhood. I miss my old friends. So I return now and then, when I can not still the longing in my heart.

The funny thing is, the moment I am in one country, I am homesick for the other.

I think I know my grandfather now. I miss him very much."

I stand in stillness, pulling myself emotionally back from the story. As I look into the faces of all those young adults, I realize that they, too, are struggling with their own emotions. I ask students to think for a minute without talking with one another. Then I ask them to draw a symbol to show what this story means to them. When I give students time to share, I see pictures of hearts torn in two, one-half labeled "home" and the other half labeled "school." I see maps indicating home and school. I see symbols representing grandparents. From some I hear a new realization that, yes, their grandparents had once been 20 years old and full of life, hope, and vigor.

Now, as I introduce the strategies we use when we comprehend—visualizing, making connections, asking questions, inferring, determining and remembering main ideas and details, synthesizing, and even using fix-up strategies—these students understand. They can clearly identify doing all those things as we shared the read-aloud. More important, we've shared a common experience and have formed an emotional bond through this book that will be the foundation of our work together as a class for the rest of the semester.

My college students have experienced the power of a good read-aloud.

— Debbie

Although there is no simple way to "inoculate" your entire class to make students susceptible to a literacy epidemic, sometimes it is more efficient and effective to work with the whole group at the same time. With a whole group, we can use the simplest and probably most powerful of all our instructional strategies: the thoughtfully chosen, engagingly read, emotionally charged read-aloud. This is one key to creating a tipping point.

Using Read-Alouds as Modeling

When we talk with teachers about using read-alouds, especially teachers above grade 3, they often look at us as though we are a bit crazy and inform us that (a) they don't have time to read to students; (b) students need the practice reading to themselves; or (c) students don't like to be read to because it is "babyish." These teachers may be picturing a teacher with a droning voice reading to a group of snoozing (or disruptive) students.

Erase that pathetic picture from your mind. Instead, picture an enthusiastic reader who exudes passion for the topic of the book and who makes the book come to life with his or her voice and facial expressions. (Remember that in *The Tipping Point*, contagiousness is a function of the messenger. Interest in a book will be contagious if the messenger makes the most of his or her role as connector, maven, and salesperson.) Picture a book that encourages students to actively make predictions, visualize events, and experience memorable events, while savoring the choice use of words and flow of sentences. (Remember that in *The Tipping Point*, "stickiness" is a function of the message itself.) Picture a setting in which the class bonds more closely because of this shared experience, and students know they'll have the opportunity to revisit the experience by rereading the book, or at least sections of it, or by making connections to it as they read related books or have related experiences. (Remember that in *The Tipping Point*, the context is critical to an epidemic's beginning and spread.)

Apprenticeship Model Chart

MODELING	SHARED PRACTICE	GUIDED PRACTICE	INDEPENDENT PRACTICE
Teacher doing; Students watching	Teacher doing; Students helping	Students doing; Teacher helping	Students doing; Teacher watching

The role of modeling in the apprenticeship model

Read-alouds hold a critical place in the apprenticeship for literacy. The range of benefits reaped from the act of reading aloud to students—all students from the preschool level through graduate school—is almost limitless.

For emergent readers, reading aloud provides a reason to become readers. When a kindergarten or first-grade teacher reads aloud *Chicka Chicka Boom Boom* by Bill Martin, Jr., clearly relishing the rhythms and rhymes in the imaginative text, students can see that reading is an enjoyable activity.

For developing readers of all ages, reading aloud provides an introduction to the thinking strategies and limitless possibilities of print. Through a read-aloud, you, the teacher, can demonstrate any and all aspects of the reading process and provide students with the modeling that is so important at the initial learning levels of the apprenticeship model. A teacher who reads aloud Steven Kellogg's *Pecos Bill*, E. B. White's *Charlotte's Web*, the "My Turn" feature from *Newsweek*, or a Shakespeare sonnet introduces his or her students to the world.

Reading aloud is a means for teachers to introduce a topic and pique the interest of all learners. Although picture books are often thought of as appropriate only for the youngest learners, the wealth of well-written, thoroughly researched picture books are a resource that can be used across all grade levels. Through a read-aloud, teachers can build background knowledge, introduce vocabulary, and expose students to the language and concepts of an area of study in a short amount of time. This applies to all areas of the curriculum and to students across grade levels. For instance, Seymour Simon's books make earth science, biology, and space immediate and enthralling. Picture book biographies like Pam Muñoz Ryan's *When Marian Sang* or David Adler's *Joe Louis: America's Fighter* make us care about people and events in the 1930s and 1940s. (For a sample lesson using *Joe Louis: America's Fighter*, see pages 58–66 in the follow-up.) Steve Jenkins' *Prehistoric Actual Size* and any of Cindy Neuschwander's Sir Cumference books make math a realm of questions and inquiry. (A wonderful resource for books listed by curriculum area is Lester Laminack and Reba Wadsworth's *Reading Aloud Across the Curriculum*.)

The same books can be used in multiple grade levels. For instance, in Stephanie Harvey and Ann Goudvis's second *Strategy Instruction in Action* video, Debbie Miller reads aloud *The Lotus Seed* by Sherry Garland to first graders. This video read-aloud demonstrates how first graders can return multiple times to a book to learn to ask questions while reading. A middle school teacher can read aloud *The Lotus Seed* as a way to introduce students to the Vietnam War, immigration issues, cultural differences, and other issues related to social studies. Many picture books deal with complex ideas that are very suitable for students in grades 3–8.

> ## Ann and Debbie's Favorite Topic-Related Read-Alouds for Older Students
>
> *The Lotus Seed* by Sherry Garland: Vietnam War, immigration, memory
>
> *Pink and Say* by Patricia Polacco: Civil War, race relations
>
> *Thank You, Sarah* by Laurie Halse Anderson: biography, U.S. history, holidays
>
> *Genius: A Photobiography of Albert Einstein* by Marfé Ferguson Delano: biography
>
> *Joe Louis: America's Fighter* by David Adler: biography, race relations, U.S. history
>
> *When Marian Sang* by Pam Muñoz Ryan: biography, race relations, U.S. history
>
> *Grandfather's Journey* by Allen Say: immigration, sense of home
>
> *The Brain and The Heart* by Seymour Simon: science, health
>
> Articles from *National Geographic's Explorer* and *Time For Kids*: science, health, and social studies topics

What is the Tipping Point in Modeling?

Those first moments we have with a class as we introduce a new topic are critical. We set the tone for our students. Each student makes quick judgments: Will this be engaging or boring? Will this be useful to me? Can I see myself getting good at this? Is the teacher interested enough to help me, or is he simply going to assign it for me to figure out? Will the immediate payoff in learning this be worth my time and effort? Will I enjoy this?

The literacy epidemic cannot spread without a successful start. Remember that you, the teacher, are the messenger described in *The Tipping Point*. As messenger, you are the connector, maven, and salesperson.

Connector: Reading aloud is a way for you to provide all students with access to information, to develop their thinking, and to encourage their participation in group discussions. This is especially important for students who struggle to read grade-level texts in the content areas. Listening to a story or an article that relates to an area of study gives all students, including those who struggle with reading, access to the language and concepts of that topic. By reading aloud to introduce students to an area of study, you broaden their thinking and questioning about that topic. A read-aloud also provides a common jumping-off point for students' writing and extended reading.

Maven: It is your knowledge of books that allows you to pick the just-right book for your students at this particular time in their studies and in their lives. You know when to read Jon Scieszka's *The Time Warp Trio* to hook reluctant readers on the fun found in books. You know to read E. L. Konigsburg's *A View From Saturday* when issues of bullying and being different are on the minds of your students. You pull out Gordon Korman's *No More Dead Dogs* when the topics on the middle school required reading list get students too emotionally overwrought. You share articles from *Newsweek*, your local newspaper, or sections of an information book when you want to pique students' interest or provide background knowledge before beginning a thorny area of study.

Salesperson: Reading aloud to students is a way for you to build community in the classroom. In *Reading Essentials,* Regie Routman says that she always starts with a read-aloud when she works with a group of children because it allows an almost instant bond to form among all the participants. We have learned the same thing. Debbie always plans a read-aloud with any teacher or student group to provide a common experience. As the anecdote at the beginning of this chapter shows, she often uses Allan Say's short but poignant *Grandfather's Journey* so that she can talk about not only reading strategies but also the effects of reading on us as human beings. We share our various emotional responses to the story, and those responses provide our common bond.

In short, reading aloud presents a forum for you and your students to interact and share within an area of instruction. When we read aloud, we model both the process of reading and our own pleasure in reading.

Developing a Planning Frame

One way for a teacher to save time is through planning. We suggest using a planning frame, a fairly simple method of lesson planning, to choose and sequence instructional methods.

- Begin by jotting down your main teaching point, the one thing you want your students to learn, no matter what, from this lesson.

- Then brainstorm possible ways to hook your students' attention and emotions to focus on that teaching point. Plan the instructional methods you'll use as part of that hook.

- Next, think of the body of the lesson. We suggest choosing two or three teaching methods that will involve students actively as you go through a miniature cycle of modeling, shared practice, guided, and independent practice. Varying the level of activity throughout the body of the lesson is important to keep the pacing engaging for students. Keep options in mind so that you can adjust the lesson to your students' responses as you teach.

- Finally, think of ways to bring closure to the lesson that will underscore your teaching point and provide invitations to use whatever you've just taught across content areas.

In essence, you're paying attention to the message and the context in your planning. (Debbie assumes she'll be a good connector and salesperson, but there are times when she needs to study ahead to be a good maven!) The following section provides a detailed overview of this planning frame. A Lesson Planning Frame on page 152 of the appendix will help to guide your thinking.

Identifying Your Content and Process Teaching Points

One of the biggest mistakes we make as teachers is in confusing teaching an idea, concept, or process with teaching a book. If we ask an upper elementary teacher what he or she is teaching, the answer is likely to be the title of a book: "Oh, we're doing *Stone Fox* now," or "I'm teaching *In the Year of the Boar and Jackie Robinson*." If we ask, "What are you teaching when you teach that book?" we often get either blank stares or exasperated looks. If you find yourself thinking, "We're teaching *Sarah, Plain and Tall* because we always teach that in the spring," then you haven't fully thought through the point of your teaching. Choosing a read-aloud to introduce a chapter book or a unit of study in social studies or science or health can help you clarify both your content-area teaching point and what you are teaching students in the area of reading, your process teaching point. The following questions will help you to focus on what you need to teach:

- *What single thing do I want my students to remember about the content?*

   Your grade-level curriculum may dictate your key content teaching point.

- *What single thing do I want my students to learn to do as readers and thinkers?*

   Your observations of your students may focus your attention on a skill or strategy that they need to learn next. Whatever you choose, it should follow logically for you and for the students from what they already know or have experienced. This will be your key process teaching point that will enable you to teach reading while you are teaching the content.

Making a Book Choice

Once you have your teaching points clearly identified, the rest of the lesson plan will flow more easily. You'll choose your read-aloud book and the instructional methods to use during the read-aloud to involve students and focus their attention. Here are some questions to ask yourself at this stage:

- *What books introduce the concepts, background knowledge, and vocabulary for my content-specific teaching point?*

- *What is my focus for the reading process? What reading process do I want my students to learn or to refine: visualizing, making connections, asking questions, inferring, synthesizing, self-monitoring, cross-checking, self-correcting? What books highlight the reading process or strategy I want to teach?*

- *Do any of the books I identified for my content goal also allow me to focus on my teaching point for reading or writing?*

Most books have many possible teaching points, so you have to be flexible in your thinking to find one that will work for you. For each book you're considering, ask yourself the following questions:

- *Can I read this book aloud in an engaging manner? (It may feel silly, but reading a page out loud in an audible voice will show you if the author's style and your mouth work together.)*

- *Am I interested in this book? Can I set a hook to engage and sustain student interest?*

- *Are there connections to other topics or subject areas I can highlight for students?*

- *Are there places to stop for think-alouds, think/pair/ shares, dramatization, and the ongoing use of graphic organizers? (A glossary of low-preparation teaching techniques for use throughout all stages of instruction can be found in the appendix on pages 153–157. We call them "desert island" teaching techniques because these strategies require so few materials that you could use them on that proverbial island.)*

- *Can I return to this book multiple times as a mentor book for the craft of writing?*

- *Can I return to this book multiple times as a touchstone across subject areas?*

- *Will this book inspire a book binge or an author binge in some of my students? Will some of my students want to read everything they can about the topic? Will some of my students want to read everything they can by the same author? Does this book provide students with a natural invitation to explore further?*

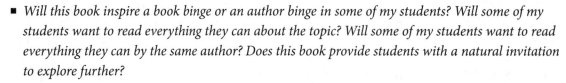

Ann and Debbie's Favorite Sources for Book Ideas

Ann's Favorites:

Book links: *Connecting Books, Libraries, and Classrooms* (American Library Association)

Professional journals: *The Reading Teacher* (IRA), *Language Arts and Voices from the Middle* (NCTE)

The Read-Aloud Handbook by Jim Trelease

Professional books I have read recently:

Still Learning to Read by Sibberson and Szymusiak

The Reading Zone by Nancie Atwell

Recommendations from other teachers, publishers' displays at conferences, and bookstore personnel

Debbie's Favorites:

Independent children's bookstores, such as Kids Ink in Indianapolis

Children's literature textbooks and software, especially *Children's Literature Briefly* by Tunnell and Jacobs

Recommendations from teachers and school and public librarians

The "People who bought this book also bought . . . " feature on Amazon.com

Workshops focusing on new children's or young adolescent books such as those offered by BER (Bureau of Educational Research)

Choosing Instructional Methods for Before, During, and After the Reading

An easy way to plan your instructional methods is to use a before/during/after format.

Before you share the read-aloud, what will you do to engage students' interest and curiosity? Will you

- pose a problem?

- do a picture walk?

- set up a graphic organizer?

- provide an emotional hook of some kind?

During the read-aloud, what will you do to keep the students engaged? Will you

- use "turn and talk" at key points?

- stop to fill in a graphic organizer?

- pose questions or ask for responses?

- make connections to knowledge from other sources related to the book?

- have students participate by reading a refrain?

- have students sketch what they are visualizing?

After you finish reading, what will you do to be sure the message has stuck? Will you

- complete a graphic organizer?

- have students do a quick-write?

- make connections to what students have learned or will learn in the content areas?

- share related materials?

- play a game using the information from the text?

- chart the reading strategies used during the reading?

- add to a running review of new information about the content area or the reading processes studied in class?

As you teach, you'll refine your lesson, constantly reflecting and testing your intuitions about your lessons in relation to your particular group of students, keeping in mind your role as the messenger who is the maven/salesperson/connector, the lesson itself as the message so you can test its "stickiness" or ease in being remembered, and what your students and classroom provide as the context. You'll follow up in some way so students *do* something with the new information to make it easier to remember.

Formats for Read-Alouds

You don't have to get into a rut as you read aloud to your students. You definitely don't want to sound like the "wah, wah, wah" of an airport loudspeaker. Here are some ways to change up your reading to keep students listening and involved.

- Teacher does a dramatic reading with changes in voices and stances to indicate change in characters. Students listen.

- Teacher reads. Students dramatize with hand motions and facial expressions (e.g., stop the reading and have students vote using thumbs-up or thumbs-down signals; have students show the expression on their faces they think a character is now wearing).

- Teacher reads. Students read the refrains. (Debbie projects refrains so everyone can see and read along. She writes the refrains herself or simply finds memorable lines for the students to repeat at intervals.)

- Teacher reads. Students talk with a buddy after teacher provides open prompt ("Say Something") or closed prompt (e.g., "What might happen next?" "What would you do if you were the character? Share your ideas with your partner.")

- Teacher reads. Students produce artwork, symbols, or questions.

- Teacher reads. Students write informal responses (e.g., predictions, connections, a written conversation with a partner).

- Teacher and students reread favorite parts of familiar stories.

Echoes Across Curricular Areas

You can use the read-aloud time to "buy" time through the integration of subject areas. A thoughtfully selected read-aloud will build background knowledge and introduce vocabulary in context. You can refer to it time and again, making connections between what appeared in the book and the topic you are studying. For example, once Debbie has read *When Marian Sang* to students, they understand some of the prejudices that existed in our country in the 1930s, while learning about Eleanor Roosevelt's actions to help others and our country's involvements prior to World War II. After reading this picture book biography, Debbie sees that students come to care about the people and the time period.

Example: A Planning Frame in Action

To see how a planning frame actually works, let's look at a lesson Debbie has taught using Seymour Simon's *The Brain: Our Nervous System*. A copy of the planning frame she completed for this lesson is shown below.

Lesson Planning Frame

What is my main teaching point, the thing I want students to know or be able to do, no matter what, at the end of this lesson?	One way to remember new vocabulary words is to actively make a personal connection to each word.
What aspects of the curriculum content knowledge and/or background knowledge covered in this lesson will students be able to apply toward other content areas?	The central nervous system's chief component is the brain. Learning about the functions of parts of the brain helps us understand the central nervous system.
Resources and materials:	The Brain by Seymour Simon

BEFORE-READING ACTIVITIES: Hooking students' interest through modeling

What I will do:	What my students will do:
Use the anticipation guide. Give 45 seconds for students to list what the brain can do. Do a picture walk through the book.	Give thumbs-up/thumbs-down. Pairs brainstorm list of what brain can do. Look at pictures and make connections to what they already know about the brain.

DURING-READING ACTIVITIES: Shared practice to guided practice to independent practice

What I will do:	What my students will do:
Read the first 4 pages aloud, having students do actions listed in the book. Model ways to make vocabulary terms memorable using props and mnemonics. Rehearse vocabulary definitions using memory aids.	Do the actions when directed by the text. Take part as actors or watch the demonstrations. Participate in the vocabulary rehearsals.

AFTER-READING ACTIVITIES: Clinching the lesson

What I will do:	What my students will do:
Make a chart with students showing ways to remember vocabulary. Instruct students to make a sample chart of their own with 4 of the words to remember the definitions. Invite students to find out more information by reading the rest of this book or by reading other related books in the classroom. Make connections to science and health texts.	Help me create the chart showing ways to remember new vocabulary. Fold paper into 4 squares. Make an example of ways to remember the vocabulary by drawing a picture, making a connection, using a mnemonic, and writing a definition. Make a note of possible book candidates for future reading.

TEACHER REFLECTION

Did my students understand the teaching point? How do I know?	What connections and invitations did I extend to encourage independent reading in content areas?

Using Seymour Simon's The Brain to provide ways to remember vocabulary and introduce the central nervous system.

✔ IDENTIFYING CONTENT AND PROCESS TEACHING POINTS

In examining the health and science curriculum for middle school grades, Debbie realized that students would be expected to understand how the central nervous system works. That curriculum is filled with key scientific vocabulary that would probably be new to students. Debbie's content teaching point is that the brain is a complex organ that affects both behavior and perception. Her process teaching point, what she's teaching students about reading, is that one way to remember new vocabulary words is to actively make a personal connection to each word.

✔ MAKING A BOOK CHOICE

There are many books, pamphlets, and Internet articles about the brain and the central nervous system, but Debbie chooses a book that focuses specifically on the brain through artwork, electron photographs, and engaging text: Seymour Simon's *The Brain*. She focuses on ways to learn and remember key vocabulary while learning information about how the brain works. The book can be used to teach other reading and writing lessons as well. A few possible teaching points for Seymour Simon's *The Brain* are shown below.

Reading Strategies, Writing Traits, and Interdisciplinary Connections Using *The Brain*

READING STRATEGIES	WRITING TRAITS	INTERDISCIPLINARY CONNECTIONS
Determining important information Focusing on ways to remember vocabulary Stopping to visualize and think about new information Using analogies to understand and remember	Using specific examples Writing with a lively voice Using specific vocabulary while providing context clues for that vocabulary Using analogies to explain or describe	Remembering key terms: *neuron, nerve, axon, dendrites, glial cells, myelin sheath, cerebrum, cerebellum, brain stem* Connecting information to health risks and diseases

A Note From Debbie

I realized that *The Brain* by Seymour Simon would take multiple days to read aloud. My purpose wasn't to share all the information in it but to help students learn a strategy for picking out key ideas and remembering new vocabulary, while introducing them to a topic they would be covering in health and science. I was "selling" them on how interesting books about their bodies could be. I found that this book was a natural, even though I used only the first few pages.

    To save planning time across groups of children and across years, I keep two 4" x 6" sticky notes attached to the inside cover of the book. One note has an overview of activities I've used before, during, and after reading this book to a group (see details on these activities on the next pages). The other one has the six-item anticipation guide I've used.

✔ CHOOSING INSTRUCTIONAL METHODS
FOR BEFORE, DURING, AND AFTER THE READING

Debbie doesn't read the entire book to students. In fact, she reads only the first four pages aloud. She uses those pages to introduce ways to remember new vocabulary and to use visualizing and making connections as strategies to understand and remember conceptually dense information. Those pages serve as an introduction to information found in both science and health books in upper elementary and middle school classes. The lively tone of Seymour Simon's book encourages audience participation during the read-aloud and demonstrates that content information can actually be exciting.

Here are before, during, and after activities Debbie has done using *The Brain* with classes from the fourth grade through the eighth grade.

Before-Reading Activities

1. I start with an agree/disagree anticipation guide. Students use hand signals to indicate their thinking. Thumbs up: they agree. Thumbs down: they disagree. Thumbs sideways: they aren't sure. I quickly make the following statements, without allowing time for discussion:

   • Your brain can do more jobs than the most powerful computer.

   • Each second, millions of signals pass through the brain.

   • The brain sends signals to *all* parts of the body.

   • Your brain stopped growing in size around the time you reached age 7.

   • There are more neurons in your brain than there are people in the world.

   • Your brain is what makes you really *you*.

   I make comments about split decisions or definite responses, but I don't reveal which statements are true. I take these statements directly from the text. When I come to them in the reading later, I nod and acknowledge the "aha!" look of recognition on students' faces, congratulating those who made the connections between the text and this prereading activity.

2. Then I have pairs of students work together for 45 seconds to list all the things their brains can do. I take another minute to quickly jot down their ideas on a chart or on the board.

3. I do a picture walk through the book, showing the diagrams, cut-away models, and close-ups from the electron microscope. This takes another minute at most. I simply want students to get the flavor of the book.

During-Reading Activities

4. Right before I start reading, I tell students they must do what the book says, just as if they were playing "Simon Says." On the first page, the aptly named author, Seymour Simon, engages the reader immediately with a set of commands: "Wiggle your toes. Scratch your nose. Take a deep breath and yawn. Decide which is your favorite food." As I read these

lines, I do the actions along with students. When it's time to choose a favorite food, I have students share with partners. Then I continue with the book: "Try to remember the last time you ate it." Again, I tell students to share with their partners. Through this process, I'm giving students practice in talking quickly with a partner and then returning their attention to the book. None of this drags, because I pace my reading and the activities to be quick.

The next page begins a section that is dense with information and new vocabulary. This is where I want to model ways to use the comprehension strategies of visualizing and making connections to remember the concepts and vocabulary. When Simon defines neurons as special messenger cells carrying signals from the brain to other parts of the body, I stop. I call two students up to the front and say they now are neurons. I hand them two addressed envelopes to hold in front of them to remind all of us that they are messenger cells. I also have written the word *neuron* in large letters on a flash card so everyone can look at it as we pronounce it. On the back of the flash card, I've written "messenger cells" and drawn a picture of an envelope.

The two students continue standing in the front of the classroom as I read. When I get to the paragraph that says that glial cells in the brain outnumber the neurons 10 to 1, I stop and look at my two "neurons." I ask the class to do some quick math: How many glial cells would it take to represent the ratio of 10 to 1? It doesn't take long for students to respond, "20."

Then I ask two more students to stand up and represent 10 glial cells each. Once those students are standing in front of the classroom, I ask what they, the glial cells, do. They look at me blankly, and I point out that the author hasn't told us yet. We had to picture the number before we knew the function. The author writes, "They [glial cells] support the neurons by supplying nutrients and other chemicals, repairing the brain after an injury, and attacking invading bacteria." I read that line, stop, and then hand the "glial cell" students a candy bar or juice box and a first-aid kit. Then I have them put their fists in the air as if they were about to box. We then reword Simon's definition: Glial cells "feed, fix, and fight" to protect and sustain the neurons. The juice box, the first-aid kit, and the boxing stance help students remember, as does the alliteration of "feed, fix, and fight." I hand those two students a flash card with "glial cells" written in large letters and a definition and set of icons on the back.

I stop again and point out the strategies that we are using to understand the text and remember the concepts and vocabulary.

Then we continue. Students' bodies become nerves with flailing dendrites and a single axon. I pull out a spool of electrical wire to show the insulation, as a way to remember the myelin sheath around the axons. I use a long piece of cording to get an approximate measure of various students' longest axons (from their tailbones to their toes). I stop periodically and review the vocabulary words by going back to the students representing the various terms. I stand by the students representing the glial cells and ask the class what they do. Everyone chants, "Feed, fix, and fight." I stand next to the students representing nerves and ask what their dendrites do. Their right arms beckon as the students say, "Give me; give me," to indicate that dendrites accept signals from other nerves. I'm modeling that we have to rehearse new vocabulary if we want to remember it.

We continue through the four target pages, finding ways to act out the vocabulary words to make them more memorable. I coach students as they try new techniques for remembering and using technical vocabulary in their reading. By the end of the four pages, I am handing the responsibility to them as a group to devise ways to remember the vocabulary. The guided practice has moved from being teacher-directed to being student-directed.

After-Reading Activities

5. We rehearse the new words and make a chart listing the ways we focused our memory on the concepts and the vocabulary (associations, dramatization, mnemonics, and visualization).

6. I have students fold a piece of paper into four sections. They work with their partner to pick four of the words or concepts we've read about. The partners' job is to draw a picture, make a connection, find a mnemonic, or write a definition that would help them remember what they've learned.

7. I stress that students have to use the information if they want to remember it. We might play a Bingo game, draw a graphic organizer, or even draft a letter to a younger student explaining how the brain works.

Once we have debriefed the content portion of the lesson, I am back in my role as reading teacher. What have students learned that they can now practice in their independent reading? I make sure they can name and explain one way to make new vocabulary memorable as a result of this lesson. The students' challenge then is to use this strategy while reading in all their content-area materials.

✔ ECHOES ACROSS CURRICULAR AREAS

I use this lesson to remind students of how they have to actively make connections and visualize to make sense of content information and new vocabulary. I also use it as my students and I talk about health issues and problems that may interfere with learning. I make sure to refer back to this lesson as we approach new topics in other content areas. As we continue in the health textbook, I'll refer back to the content of Seymour Simon's book. Whenever we come across new vocabulary in other content areas, I'll prompt students to think of a way they can visualize the meaning of the word by making a personal connection to it in some way. I don't have to reread *The Brain* to do this. All I have to do is refer back to the day I read the book and then ask for suggestions based on that activity as we approach new vocabulary challenges.

Change Over Time and Across Developmental Levels

Reading aloud to older students may look very similar to what they experienced in the primary grades, but this is deceptive. The purposes for reading aloud to students change over time, as do the types of texts you use.

The following chart will help you think of new uses for read-alouds and affirm the use of picture books for older students.

Developmental Chart for Read-Alouds

	GRADES K–2	GRADES 2–4	GRADES 4–6	GRADES 6–9
Concept books (ABC or numbers)	To develop and extend students' knowledge of concepts	To recognize and adapt writing patterns		
Picture books (stand-alone)	To develop vocabulary, concepts, sense of story, and understanding of reading process	To develop vocabulary, concepts, cognitive skills for comprehension, and craft of writing	To introduce and develop ability to form an opinion and to practice art of group discussion	
Picture books as preface to units		To provide background knowledge	To stimulate interest in topic; to provide background knowledge, language, and basic concepts	To stimulate interest in topic; to provide background knowledge, language, and basic concepts
Simple chapter books	To develop listening comprehension of story read over time	To analyze story structure and recognize fundamental literary elements	To participate in discussion of book	
Poetry	Exposure to beauty and rhythm and rhyme of language	To experience use of language for imagery	To inspire reflection and deep thinking	To use as model in writing poetry
Complex short stories			To learn value of rereading	To develop comprehension and composition skills
Complex chapter books		To preview a text to make connections to the text	To keep track of multiple story characters and change of setting	To persevere in reading difficult text
Quips, jokes, or cartoons	To entertain and practice oral reading with short text	To detect surprise, exaggeration, and make inferences	To infer, to play with language, to make connections to current or historical events	To recognize irony, parody, or satire; to understand political references
Humorous or odd short articles		To entertain	To pique curiosity; to make connections	To analyze types of humor; to recognize voice in writing
Essays		To learn about this genre	To form an opinion; to see power of writing	To use as model for writing essays
News articles	To see writing as communication; to develop a sense of community	To gain information about current events	To connect current events to history, math, and science	To use as model for writing news articles
Speeches			To understand power of language to influence	To use as model for writing speeches
Audio productions	To develop art of listening	To access text above one's reading level	To use as model for oral presentations	
Student-written text	To discover joy of being an author and to develop fluency	To build classroom community; to appreciate writing of peers	To provide and receive constructive feedback	To recognize students as capable authors

Planning & Managing Effective Reading Instruction Across the Content Areas

Possible Solutions to Management and Behavioral Issues

Scenario 1: This classroom is an observer's nightmare. The eighth graders are whispering to their neighbors or have their heads on their desks. No one seems to be listening to the teacher who is plowing through a short story from the three-inch-thick literature book. She stops frequently, first to reprimand John for having his head down, next to tell Celeste to move away from Sarah, then to give a detention to Maurice who has pronounced in a loud whisper, "This is stupid." When the teacher does read, her pace is rapid, and her vocal tone is similar to the whiny tone of her reprimands. She finishes with an audible sigh, puts the book on her desk, and tells students to start to work on their homework from the grammar book. She sidles over to Debbie and says with a note of triumph in her voice, "I told you they don't listen. That's why I don't waste class time reading aloud to these kids. They think it's babyish, and besides, they need to practice reading on their own."

Scenario 2: In another class, a middle-aged teacher reads aloud. Her seventh graders pay rapt attention, hanging on her every word. Some cradle their chins in their hands and listen with faraway looks as she reads Dickens's A Christmas Carol. *The teacher stops periodically and describes what she is seeing in her mind as she reads about the scanty meal that makes up the Cratchett's Christmas dinner. She rereads Dickens's words describing the inadequate quantity of food as well as the words that tell us how special this meal is. The teacher reminisces about her own Christmas pasts and invites students to remember family celebrations. Her voice is warm and animated. She speeds up in the parts that pile on details; she slows to savor particular images. The characters speak through her voice. None of us, students or observer, wants this time to end.*

How can there be such a difference in student responses just one hallway and one grade level apart? In the first scenario, the teacher obviously sees reading aloud as a chore and a waste of time. In the second scenario, the teacher clearly sees reading aloud as an opportunity to connect students with a bygone time and convince them that Dickens is not only accessible but also fascinating.

Clearly, you want to be like the teacher in the second scenario. As in any classroom event, however, the best-laid plans for a read-aloud can run amuck. What can you do when things just don't seem to go right during a read-aloud? Before you decide to just throw out the book, and especially before you abandon the strategy, take some time to think through what went wrong and why. Generally, there are three areas where the problem might lie: (1) you—and how you are conducting the read-aloud (the messenger); (2) the text or materials you are using (the message); or (3) students' engagement (the context).

Debbie's Favorite Picture Book Biographies for Modeling Comprehension Strategies and Highlighting the Craft of Writing

Your Turn

1. Where do you find new book titles to use in your class? Where does the most avid reader in your building find titles? **2.** When do you find time during the school year to read children's books? Over breakfast? Waiting for your own children at music lessons or sports practices? Before bed?

Adler, David A.	*Joe Louis: America's Fighter*
Adler, David	*The Babe & I*
Aliki	*William Shakespeare & the Globe*
Anderson, William	*Pioneer Girl: The Story of Laura Ingalls Wilder*
Bildner, Phil	*Shoeless Joe & Black Betsy*
Bridges, Ruby	*Through My Eyes*
Burleigh, Robert	*Flight*
Cline-Ransome, Lesa	*Major Taylor: Champion Cyclist*
Cooney, Barbara	*Eleanor*
Cooney, Barbara	*Emily*
Farris, Christine King	*My Brother Martin*
Freedman, Russell	*The Voice That Challenged a Nation*
Freedman, Russell	*Lincoln: A Photobiography*
Golenbock, Peter	*Teammates: Jackie Robinson and "Pee Wee" Reese*
Grimes, Nikki	*Talkin' About Bessie*
Harness, Cheryl	*Mark Twain and the Queens of the Mississippi*
Haskins, Jim	*Delivering Justice: W. W. Law and the Fight for Civil Rights*
Hilliard, Richard	*Godspeed, John Glenn*
Keating, Frank	*Will Rogers*
Kerley, Barbara	*Walt Whitman: Words for America*
MacLeod, Elizabeth	*Marie Curie: A Brilliant Life*
Martin, Jacqueline Briggs	*Snowflake Bentley*
McCully, Emily Arnold	*Squirrel and John Muir*
Moss, Marissa	*Mighty Jackie: The Strike-Out Queen*
O'Connor, Jane	*If the Walls Could Talk: Family Life at the White House*
Perdomo, Willie	*Visiting Langston*
Pinkney, Andrea Davis	*Duke Ellington*
Pringle, Laurence	*American Slave, American Hero: York of the Lewis and Clark Expedition*
Ray, Deborah Kogan	*The Flower Hunter: William Bartram, America's First Naturalist*
Roth, Susan	*Do, Re, Mi: If You Can Read Music, Thank Guido d'Arezzo*
Rumford, James:	*Seeker of Knowledge: The Man Who Deciphered Egyptian Hieroglyphs*
Ryan, Pam Muñoz	*Amelia and Eleanor Go For a Ride*
Ryan, Pam Muñoz	*When Marian Sang*
Selznick, Brian	*The Houdini Box*
Shaughnessy, Dan	*The Legend of the Curse of the Bambino*
Sis, Peter	*Starry Messenger*
Smith, Lane	*John, Paul, George & Ben*
St. George, Judith	*So You Want To Be an Explorer*
St. George, Judith	*So You Want To Be an Inventor*
St. George, Judith	*So You Want To Be President*
Stanley, Diane	*Peter the Great*
Warren, Andrea	*Orphan Train Rider: One Boy's True Story*

✔ PROBLEMS WITH THE MESSENGER

Address and assess your role in a read-aloud that does not go well by reflecting on your reading of the text. Ask yourself the following questions:

- *Did I preread the text, preparing to lead students' through thinking about the author's message?*

- *Did I plan for the amount of text I'd read in one session? If not the whole text, what part of the text would be best to read aloud?*

- *Did I read with expression and enthusiasm, engaging my students in the story or text?* (Try tape-recording your reading aloud and see how it sounds. You don't have to be a great actor or actress, but the words do have to come to life through your voice.)

- *Did my facial expressions and body language help convey the text?* (If you are brave, you can videotape yourself as you do a read-aloud. I (Debbie) must admit that I've changed hairstyles and thrown out favorite clothes after seeing myself in a teaching video. It can be a humbling experience at any age!)

- *Did I stop often enough or too often to assist students in thinking about the message, without interrupting their train of thought? Did I stop in the right places?*

By prereading a text, you become familiar with the language, concepts, and cognitive strategies demanded by it. This prepares you to be able to both read the text fluently, conveying meaning with your voice, and to model the thinking that students will need to do to understand the author's message. During this preparation phase, you can devise a plan for when to stop and engage students in a discussion about the text.

✔ PROBLEMS WITH THE MESSAGE

The text itself might be the cause of an unsuccessful read-aloud. Consider the following when choosing and/or evaluating a text for reading aloud:

- *Is the subject of the text of interest to my students? If not, what personal hook can I set to help students develop an interest?*

- *Does the author present the story/information in a way that will engage listeners?*

- *Is the writing style conducive to reading aloud?* Think about the vocabulary, point of view, syntax, placement and size of any pictures and how you plan to share them with the group, variation in the length of sentences, and even the places where the page turns. (One of the best placements of a page turn is in *Rumpelstiltskin's Daughter* by Diane Stanley. Watch students' expressions as the boorish king tells the clever girl that he plans to marry her despite her failure in providing him with real gold. I guarantee you that all the children will stop breathing for a second until you turn the page and read the girl's response.)

- *Is there another text for my teaching point that I could use that would be more appropriate for my students?*

✔ PROBLEMS WITH THE CONTEXT

Finally, the problem might center on the students themselves. This does not necessarily mean they are being disruptive. In order to engage your students in listening well to a read-aloud, you must consider what was noted above regarding teacher and text. Then you can look at what your students bring to the lesson. First, you need to think of their physical comfort and needs:

- *Have they already been sitting inactive for a period of time?* If so, don't start a read-aloud until they've had a chance to move around a bit and talk.

- *Is the time scheduled for the read-aloud right before an anticipated break for lunch, recess, physical education, or even the end of the period for middle school students?* If so, reschedule it.

- *Are students located where they can see you and hear your voice without straining?* (I [Debbie] often work in a school with extremely loud air handlers. If I'm standing in the back of the room, I cannot hear the teacher clearly, despite my efforts. I know I have middle-aged ears, but if I'm having difficulty, the ENL students and ADHD students in that back row are certainly going to struggle.)

- *Are students uncomfortable where they are seated? If they are on the floor, are they too crowded or are they next to a wiggly child? If they are at their desks, are they too far from you?* If so, move throughout the read-aloud so that all students are close to the book and you, the reader, at some point.

Another important consideration is the students' prior experience. Do they know what they are supposed to be doing as they listen? At a Reading Recovery conference several years ago, kindergarten teachers were bemoaning the fact that children were rolling on the floor, seemingly unengaged by even the most dramatic read-alouds. The ensuing discussion uncovered the fact that few, if any, of the students had ever been read to prior to coming to school. They didn't know how to listen or how to think about what was being read. The teachers at that conference began planning how to teach students to listen. They realized that they needed to provide explicit modeling and guided practice. They also needed to start with small amounts of listening time for students and then follow up with targeted praise for even approximations of expected responses. We can't expect newcomers to read-alouds to know how to listen to our voices any more than many of us would know how to listen to and appreciate a Wagner opera. To be honest, I [Debbie] still get a bit squirmy and distracted when listening to long, unfamiliar symphony pieces. I need to start with short, easily accessible pieces for both the symphony and the opera because I have little background experience in these areas.

Also, consider student responses and activity during a read-aloud. You want them to be actively engaged in listening, thinking about, and reacting to the story. Before the read-aloud begins, give students a purpose for listening and encourage them to write, draw, ask questions, or stop and discuss the text as you read to them. Consider the following questions:

- *What is my instructional rationale for choosing the text?*

- *What purpose will I give students for listening?*

- *How will students respond to the text using this purpose as a lens for their thinking?*
- *How can I encourage students to ask questions, share thoughts, and interact with each other as they listen to the text?*

By using "Say Something" or "think/pair/share," you can stop reading and have students reflect for a minute and then share their thinking about the text with a partner. Asking students to draw pictures they "see" in their heads or to fill in a graphic organizer about the characters or events in the story are good ways to engage them and organize their thinking and response to a text.

To Sum it Up

Through read-alouds, you can develop and extend students' habits of mind that are so important in a literate life. Sitting together in a comfortable corner of the classroom and hearing wonderful stories read aloud helps students appreciate the joys and feel the gratification of frequent reading. Reading aloud provides all students, regardless of reading ability, the means to become engaged in a story, relate to characters, feel the emotional impact of events and the struggles of problem-solving portrayed in the story, and have vicarious experiences that would otherwise be inaccessible to them. By choosing books that are well written and that deal with the breadth of human experience, you broaden students' views of the world and their ability to relate to and empathize with others. What better way for students to begin to understand the pain and injustice of racial prejudice endured by Joe Louis or Marian Anderson than by listening to their stories unfold in the pages of a well-crafted, illustrated biography? When you read aloud to students, you convey to them the understanding that they are a part of a larger human community and that, despite many differences on the outside, we have much in common on the inside.

In the follow-up to this chapter, we walk through another sample lesson using a picture book biography of Joe Louis to introduce the era of the 1930s to an upper elementary class. You'll see how the planning frame works in conjunction with the "desert island" strategies to focus on teaching points for both the content area and reading process. The shared experience of the read-aloud provides the model for our apprentice learners to improve their reading while learning content.

You are the messenger. You connect your students to the world of information. You are the maven, the trusted and knowledgeable guide. You "sell" your students on reading and writing. When you inoculate the whole class through the shared read-aloud, you provide a common incubation period and reference point for a literacy epidemic.

A Closer Look at Interactive Read-Alouds
Lesson Planning Logistics

Two complementary processes are at work as we plan our teaching for a particular group of students. First, we want to start a literacy epidemic. We want all of our students to become avid readers, especially in our target content area, because of their work in our classes. Second, we know the best way to teach students as individuals is to use an apprenticeship model in which we model for them and then gradually turn the responsibility of reading to them through shared, guided, and independent practice. These two processes come together most naturally here, through interactive read-alouds.

Your planning will echo these dual processes. Because you're starting a literacy epidemic, you have to plan for the messenger, the message, and the context. You also have to keep your big-picture content-area goals in mind. You plan your read-aloud to enhance your students' understanding of your content area.

Once you've identified your content and process teaching points, all your instructional decisions should echo them throughout the interactive read-aloud. Now you face a potentially daunting question: With those teaching points in mind, what teaching methods will work best for this book and for these students? You don't have hours to plan and research each lesson, so what are possible shortcuts? Debbie uses a list of easy-to-use, low-preparation teaching methods over and over, adapting them for her students and the focus text. She calls them "desert island" strategies because she could teach reading on the proverbial desert island with them (see pages 153–157 in the appendix). Feel free to use them as you walk through these steps in lesson planning. More important, add your own favorites and new discoveries to the list. Having the list of teaching methods in front of you as you plan helps keep your lessons fresh. The list will remind you of possibilities so you can put different combinations together, based on your teaching points and the students' need for change in the daily routine.

Now, let's walk through lesson planning logistics for interactive read-alouds. Here are questions to ask yourself about each stage of the read-aloud lesson.

✔ BEFORE READING

1. How will I engage students' curiosity and interest before I begin to read this book?

- Picture walk?

- Prediction riddle?

- Open-ended graphic organizer?

- Anticipation guide?

- Agree/disagree exercise?

- Probable passage exercise (Kylene Beers's idea from *When Kids Can't Read What Teachers Can Do*)?

2. Will I be able to keep this warm-up activity brief and to the point—no more than 5–10 minutes?

✔ DURING READING

3. Where are the most effective places to stop reading to model thinking aloud? What will I say to keep the focus on my teaching point?

4. Where will I stop to ask students to "Say Something" to their partner?

5. What questions will I want to use as prompts for student thinking? Will these questions keep the focus on my teaching point?

6. Will it be helpful for students to use a graphic organizer to help them keep track of information?

7. Where will I stop so students can help me make predictions? Connections? Inferences?

8. Does the book offer opportunities to invite students to dramatize a situation or act out vocabulary?

✔ AFTER READING

9. How much silence will I allow so students can savor the ending?

10. How will I refocus students' attention on my key teaching point?

- Will we return to the anticipation guide I used to introduce the book?

- Will we complete a graphic organizer?

- Will we make new connections and ask new questions?

- Will we find spots to reread and revisit in the text?

- Will students write their responses individually before sharing them with a buddy and then sharing them in a small group?

You can see in Chapter 2 how these questions worked to help Debbie plan the read-aloud for *The Brain* (see pages 44–49). She found the anticipation guide really helpful to grab interest before reading as well as to provide familiar "islands" of information as she read the book aloud. The students were really pleased to hear lines from the text that confirmed their initial ideas. Debbie and her students then returned to it at the end to see if they all agreed or disagreed with the same statements.

✔ REVISITING THE TEXT

11. What connections will I make throughout the remainder of the school year to this shared reading experience today? (Think of possibilities from Ellin Keene and Susan Zimmerman's *Mosaic of Thought*: text-to-self, text-to-text, text-to-world.)

- Topic?

- Characterization?

- Background information?

- Organizational structure?

- Sentence fluency?

- Word choice?

Debbie usually makes an anchor chart of the ways that her class remembered key vocabulary. That becomes a useful reference tool throughout the year as students encounter new vocabulary, regardless of subject area. *The Brain* also becomes an example of ways to make potentially dry information come to life through examples and analogies. Think about how you can use a graphic organizer or an anchor chart to remind students of the reading lessons they've learned through your read-aloud.

In the sample lesson that follows, Debbie shows how careful planning has helped her use the picture book *Joe Louis, America's Hero* successfully across multiple grade levels, from grade 5 to college.

Sample Lesson:
Joe Louis, America's Fighter by David Adler

Writing workshop advocates recommend choosing mentor books that are models of effective writing with a depth that allows the reader to return to the book over and over for new lessons. That picture is not complete. We can choose mentor texts that also allow us to model complex comprehension strategies. The trick is to choose well-written books that do both. We can use these texts to model comprehension in action *and* call attention to clear instances of good writing. For example, I've been using David Adler's *Joe Louis: America's Fighter* across grade levels to model making connections, visualizing, inferring, asking questions, and synthesizing. I also use this book to highlight instances of wonderful writing: sentence fluency, the use of an effective analogy, selecting the perfect word. Finally, I use Adler's book to focus on a particular reading strategy: determining important ideas and organizing them in a way to make them memorable.

We know that kids can't learn if they aren't attending. Using a book with an emotional hook and a problem to solve can involve them both emotionally and intellectually. Adler's *Joe Louis America's Fighter* engages students emotionally, while putting them in the context of African-American life during the Depression and World War II. In other words, the book provides a way to model comprehending and writing strategies while engaging students' interest. At the same time, students are building background knowledge about American and world history, making connections to other content areas. By choosing a mentor text that fosters the use of comprehension strategies, models good writing, establishes an emotional or intellectual hook, and provides cross-curricular connections, we have made the first step in providing an efficient and effective literacy lesson.

A mentor text is a powerful piece whose content and writing style touch us intellectually and emotionally. It is called a mentor text because it continues to teach us on many levels. The following chart demonstrates the ways that the book, *Joe Louis, America's Fighter*, can be used not only for the initial demonstration lesson, but also for subsequent lessons in reading, writing, and social studies. Once you've identified your teaching point for a lesson, you can look at your mentor texts for the best one to use or revisit as you complete your planning frame.

As Ann and I have mentioned before, we spend time to save time. If we hook students' interest in a mentor book on our first presentation, we can refer to it over and over throughout the rest of the school year, rereading pertinent passages, reminding students of connections made, using it as the foundation for new learning across subject areas. But we don't have to spend as much time reading it as we did the first time. A reminder and an invitation to reconnect with the book are enough.

However, it's not enough to simply read a book, no matter how wonderful, and hope it works its magic. If we want to use it as a mentor text, we need some strategic lesson planning and an

Mentor Text: *Joe Louis, America's Fighter* by David Adler		
READING COMPREHENSION SCAFFOLDS AND STRATEGIES MODELED DURING THE READ-ALOUD	**WRITING TECHNIQUES HIGHLIGHTED**	**CONNECTIONS TO CONTENT AREAS AND OTHER READING**
Picturing timelines Using picture previews Setting purposes Asking questions Using a graphic organizer to remember key ideas Say something (Discuss briefly with a partner) Making predictions Making connections with known information Reading fluently, especially changing the pacing of reading to reflect the action in the story Reading with expression	Sentence fluency, especially a long sentence followed by one that "packs a punch" in very few words Parallelism of sentences throughout a paragraph Choosing an analogy or a word for effect Using quotations from others for effect Presentation: strategic use of page breaks	The Black Migration The Great Depression Everyday life in the 1920s and 1930s for African-American families The use of sports, especially boxing, as a "way out" for minorities in America World War II and black Americans' involvement Comparisons to other historic figures (Muhammad Ali for boxing, Marian Anderson for the 1930s African-American experience)

Sample sheet for mentor text

engaging presentation. To save planning time in the future, I have a large sticky note inside the front cover of each of my mentor books. On it, I list the instructional strategies I've used successfully in the past and any reminders of questions or possible pitfalls in using that book.

Based on my notes in *Joe Louis, America's Fighter* here's what has worked for me in sharing this book in a classroom setting. This lesson takes about 35 minutes. Pairs of students work together as "study buddies" when I offer either a question or an open-ended prompt that gives them the opportunity to "say something."

✔ BEFORE READING

I stretch a timeline across the front of the room and have students quickly draw symbols on 3" x 3" index cards to help me mark landmark personal events in the 20th century, including family birthdates and other events with special connections. I add my own birth year, my daughter's 1992 birthdate, and the birthdates of my mother (1906) and my father (1914). (If the students are perplexed about the spread in dates, I let them know I'm adopted.) We record the two world wars, the invention of the Model T, the moon landing, movies (*The Wizard of Oz* in 1939, for example), and anything else of importance that we can remember. I have copies of reference books, including the *Junior Chronicle of the Twentieth Century* to help us if we get stuck. The pacing of this activity is quick—no more than 5 to 8 minutes—with students getting up to add to the timeline as they think of something and I've acknowledged their idea. Through this activity, I'm modeling how to make personal connections to information.

After we complete the timeline, I tell students that we are going to share the story of a very famous man who lived in the 20th century, a boxer. Most classes immediately guess that I'm referring to Muhammad Ali. I counter that some people think the man we will read about is even greater than Ali. The looks of shock and disbelief tell me that students are already curious.

I display the book and give partners 30 seconds to brainstorm all they can about the man on

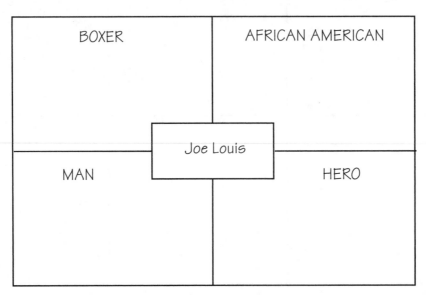

Joe Louis, America's Fighter *graphic organizer*

the cover. To show what I noticed from the cover and to set a purpose for reading, I do a think-aloud. Next, I present a simple graphic organizer on a transparency or draw it on chart paper. My purpose is to find out more about this man in each of four areas.

✔ DURING READING

The book starts with a chronology of Joe Louis's life, starting with his birth in 1914 and ending with his death in 1981. Rather than reading all the dates, I show the span on our timeline and note that Joe Louis and my father were born in the same year. I take about 30 seconds to make personal connections to family stories about what life was like when my father was young. Then I note that Joe Louis was a black man born in Alabama. I model through a think-aloud how I move from thinking about a personal connection to my father to what I know about the world of the South and sharecroppers in 1914. Then I turn to the first picture in the book, a horse-drawn cart filled with bags of cotton and a man in the foreground picking cotton, which confirms my connections.

I read aloud the first page, about how Joseph Louis Barrow was the seventh of eight children, how the family lived without running water or electricity, and how Joe's father was committed to the Searcy State Hospital for the Colored Insane in 1916. I stop. I let the words sink in. Both *colored* and *insane* sound shocking. I talk about the author's use of language from that time period to put us in the historic context of the South in the early twentieth century even though the words seem demeaning to us now. Then the students and I confirm that Joe would have been 2 years old when his father went away and that he had a younger sibling. I give study buddies 30 seconds to make predictions about what Joe's mother, Lillie, would do to take care of her family under these conditions. I wander around the room, eavesdropping on conversations, calling out key ideas as I hear them: the older children will be put to work; some of the kids will be sent to live with relatives; Lillie will have to go to work; they'll have to leave the farm if they can't do the sharecropping.

Then I turn the page and continue to read aloud. Joe's mother remarries, and the family moves to Detroit, Michigan, in 1926. I stop again and mention that I know from reading other books about Joe Louis that his mother married a man with an equally large family. As students stare at me incredulously, I invite the next connection: "What was happening in Detroit in 1926 that would attract the family?" Automobiles. I make another quick connection to what I know about the great Black Migration, adding details about black families being locked up in Southern jails at train time to keep them from leaving—yet they found their way north anyway. Then the study buddies have another 30 seconds to discuss this prompt: "How will life be different for 12-year-old Joe?" As I continue to read aloud, the page confirms some of their ideas and introduces others. The author mentions that Joe had a job delivering ice. I make connections to my mother always referring to the refrigerator as the "icebox" and explain what the term means. I pantomime what it would be like to carry blocks of ice with big tongs and speculate about the strength a 12-year-old would need to do that job.

At this point, I stop reading and ask, "What information about Joe Louis can we put on our graphic organizer?" We know a little about Joe's personal history, so we can add those details under the category "man." We can't say anything about Joe Louis as a boxer or a hero yet, so those quadrants remain blank. Some students instruct me to write information about the plight Joe shared with other African-Americans of the time, e.g., sharecropping and the Black Migration, and I write those details in the "African-American" category.

On the next page, Adler introduces Joe's initiation into boxing, providing the anecdote that for his first fight he wrote his name so large he didn't have room for his last name. From then on, he was simply "Joe Louis." I invite students to make a quick personal connection: "Have any of you ever written your name so large it didn't fit on a sheet of paper? What would your name be if you suddenly lost your last name? How would you feel?"

The next page starts with Joe's first amateur fight. I stop in midsentence and have students make a prediction as to who will win. We do a quick vote: thumbs up if they think Joe wins, thumbs down if they think he loses. Usually the students' predictions are mixed. Then I read the rest of the sentence. Joe Louis's fight is against Johnny Miler, a member of the Olympic boxing team. We vote again. Almost all the students have their thumbs down now. Then I read Adler's account of how Joe was knocked down seven times before he lost and how his mother cried and asked him to stop boxing. As an aside, I mention that I learned from other books that Joe's mother had been giving him money for violin lessons but that he'd used the money to rent a locker at the gym. His mother found out when he came home bloodied from the fight. We take another 30 seconds for the study buddies to make some predictions about what will happen now that Joe's mother knows. Again, I eavesdrop and call out key ideas I overhear: his mother will be really mad; he can't stop boxing or the story would end. I read the next page so students know Joe tried to stay away from the gym but couldn't. They learn he won his next 14 fights, and 50 of his 54 amateur fights, before becoming a professional.

We stop again to add information to our graphic organizer. Now we have information about Joe Louis as a boxer as well as more information about him as a man. Some students highlight character traits at this point, too, noting Joe's persistence in getting up seven times when fighting Miler. I also ask the study buddies to discuss the difference between an amateur fight and a professional fight. Again, I call out what I overhear, and then continue to read: "On July 4, 1934, twenty-year-old Joe Louis had his first professional fight. It was big-time boxing, with a paycheck. The fight was set to last ten rounds, but Louis knocked Jack Kracken out in the first round!"

Now I pause to model the inferences I'm making: if Joe is fighting professionally, he can use the money to support his family, especially in the 1930s during the Depression. If Joe knocked the man out in the first round, he must really be good. Maybe he was supposed to make the fight last ten rounds, but he was too excited because it was his first fight, so he didn't hold back.

That leads to the next page, a description of the Great Depression and its effects, especially on African-Americans. Adler introduces the racial discrimination and tensions Joe faced in those times. The page ends with the information that Joe is to fight a white former heavyweight champion, Primo Carnera, in Yankee Stadium, just outside Harlem. I pause to ask: "What would you do if you were the police commissioner and this fight was scheduled?" Again, 30 seconds at most is all that is needed for study buddies to imagine the danger and the police response. I turn the page and confirm their responses. Adler writes that the police commissioner sent more than a thousand police officers to Yankee Stadium to control the 60,000 fans. I use my best Howard Cosell voice to read the ring announcer's words, "Regardless of race, creed, or color, let us all say, may the better man emerge victorious." (For you younger readers, Howard Cosell was a famous sports announcer with a distinctive voice and cadence.)

We take a quick thumbs-up/thumbs-down vote: Will Joe win? Most students have their thumbs up. They are rooting for Joe. The next page confirms their predictions. We take a minute to add to the graphic organizer. On the next page, we learn that Joe Louis married Marva Trotter and took her on their wedding night to Yankee Stadium to see him fight. I lower the book and inject a personal response to that piece of information.

Then I continue reading aloud with the account of Joe's fight with Max Baer. (If I'm with a class of TV-Land fans, I mention *The Beverly Hillbillies* and that the man who plays Jethro is the son of Max Baer. For some students, that piece of information makes them suddenly realize we are talking about real people, not story characters.)

I do not show the picture when I turn to the next page. Instead, I read of Joe's scheduled fight against the German fighter Max Schmeling. I refer to our timeline so students can see that this fight is just prior to World War II. I read Adler's words: "Suddenly, this fight wasn't a black fighter against a white one. It was an American against a German. For many people, both blacks *and* whites, Joe Louis was fighting their fight." Study buddies have 30 seconds to talk and predict what will happen. We take a thumbs-up/thumbs-down vote. Most classes are confident of Joe's victory. Then I show the picture of the fight. Joe is stretched out, facedown on the canvas as the ref counts him out. Students' gasps are usually audible at this point.

We stop for the study buddies to talk: How will Joe feel? What will he do? After 30 seconds, I show the picture on the next page. The illustrator, Terry Widener, has captured the despair Joe felt. There is usually a moment of silence in the classroom as everyone shares in his grief. Then, as I read about how people in Germany celebrated Joe's defeat, the students' shared sense of wounded pride is palpable. They are living Joe's life through this picture book. I read on, about Joe's upcoming bout with the world heavyweight champion, James J. Braddock, on June 22, 1937. I mention the movie *Cinderella Man,* and briefly describe Braddock's struggle to become the champion. Students pause, talk, and then signal with their thumbs if they think Joe will win. I read the next paragraphs telling of Braddock's defeat. Then we fill out additional information on the graphic organizer about the new world's heavyweight champion, Joe Louis.

The last paragraph on that page, however, changes the mood in the classroom from one of celebration to one of pure determination. Adler notes that the German press declared that Max Schmeling was still the world champion. I ask students what Joe could do. In some classes, it almost becomes a chant, "Rematch, rematch!"

The next two pages set up the scene of the rematch: anti-Nazi demonstrators, 70,000 fight fans, radio broadcasts in four languages, and the words of Joe Louis: "This isn't just one man against another. It is the good old U.S.A. versus Germany."

The study buddies put their heads together: How will the crowd react? What will happen in the fight? What will go through Joe's mind? What will Schmeling be thinking? In one class in which I worked, two students acted out the fight scene. The class cheered wildly when "Joe" made his entrance, hands clasped overhead in a champion's pose, and they hooted and rumbled when "Max" came out. Designated paper wad throwers launched their missiles at him.

Then I read Adler's account of the bout with the quick pacing of a radio announcer calling a prize fight. When I read the words, "In just 124 seconds, Joe Louis had beaten Max Schmeling," the classroom usually erupts in cheers.

I read the next short paragraphs slowly: the first paragraph to underscore Joe Louis as hero, the second to glory in language and history:

> "Both black and white Americans everywhere celebrated. Joe Louis was their hero.
>
> 'The decline of Nazi prestige,' one reporter wrote, 'began with a left hook.'"

We pause to add to our graphic organizer. There is so much to put under the categories of boxer and hero, man, and African-American. The students look at me as though the story has ended, and they are satisfied with their hero. To re-engage them in Joe's story, I pose the following question: "With World War II underway, will Joe enlist or stay home?" Some students share their knowledge of Cassius Clay's decision to convert to Islam and become the conscientious objector, Muhammad Ali. Some argue that Joe would be "stupid" to go to war. Some argue that there is no way that he couldn't become involved somehow.

I turn the page. Widener's illustration of Joe Louis in an army uniform in front of an American flag says it all. I read about his confidence in joining the fight, of his giving all the proceeds of two title fights while he was in the army to the Navy and Army Relief Funds. We stop and add more to the graphic organizer.

I continue to read aloud, sharing that Joe continued fighting after the war, winning all of his championship fights. Then I read my two favorite sentences in the book that highlight sentence fluency, putting, of course, a slight pause between the two:

> "In 1949, Joe Louis retired from boxing, undefeated as world champion.
>
> In 1950, he was back."

We stop, and I pose the following questions: "Why would Joe continue fighting? How old is too old for an athlete? What happens when there is no more money coming in?"

I continue reading. We learn that despite his efforts, Joe couldn't regain his title. He had his last match against Rocky Marciano. Adler, again, has picked a quotation that highlights powerful writing:

> "'The record books will say it was Marciano who beat Joe,' one reporter wrote, 'but everybody knows it was age.'"

That sentence is followed by Adler's wonderful use of parallelism to end the book:

> "In the tough years of the 1930s, when African Americans needed a hero, they had Joe Louis. During the tough years of World War II, when all Americans needed a hero, they had Joe Louis, too. Many fight fans, black and white, said Joe Louis was the greatest heavyweight champion ever."

The book has cast a spell on the class. Everyone has been transported to the early years of the 20th century to experience Joe Louis's rise to fame. Jeff Wilhelm talks of readers having to *become* the book to comprehend it in all its richness. I have yet to use this book with a group of students from grade 5 through college who don't become immersed in the story.

Finally, I read Adler's author's notes, listening for the audible sigh when the students learn that Schmeling saved children from the Nazis during the war and later became friends with Joe. We return to our graphic organizer, filling in more details. But there are still questions to be answered; for example, what happened to Joe Louis between his retirement and his death in 1981?

✔ AFTER READING

We have spent about 30 minutes on the book at this point. I've modeled thinking strategies while reading aloud, used a graphic organizer for keeping track of information, and celebrated instances of good writing. In some classes, if I have more time, I follow up with an article about Joe Louis from the Internet, a source most students frequently use. I briefly talk about the importance of finding a credible site (I use an article from the *Detroit News* archives) and again set a purpose for my reading. If I am highlighting making connections and asking questions as reading strategies, I jigsaw the article so each set of study buddies gets two or three paragraphs. To focus on the positive act of making connections, each set of study buddies reads through its section, using a highlighter to mark the information they *already* know. The study buddies also search for clues as to what Joe did after he retired from boxing and why that may have happened. Next to these clues, they put an asterisk.

As I walk around the room, I see huge portions of each section highlighted in yellow. These students, who knew so little about the 1930s just 30 minutes before, are now experts on the time period and one of its leading athletes. As I stop and talk to pairs of students, they are eager to share new tidbits of information about Joe Louis. Even struggling readers appear to have no trouble comprehending the Internet article. Their background knowledge, coupled with the help of a buddy, support the new reading.

After about 5 minutes, we share. I add their new information to the graphic organizer. We bemoan Joe's financial difficulties and are thankful for the friends who supported him and paid for his medical care. We add key information about Joe and his world to our timeline. In this way, I model how readers need to stop and think about what they have learned, adding new knowledge to what they already know about the world.

I also want to model the importance of processing knowledge:

- *What have we experienced today as readers that will make us better readers in the future?* We have made connections, asked questions, paced our reading to match the action in the story, stopped throughout to think and predict, become emotionally involved.

- *What have we learned about writing that we can use as writers?* We've highlighted the use of quotations from background information, pacing, sentence fluency, word choice.

- *Most important, what have we learned about finding important information and organizing it in a way to make it memorable? Can we use this technique when reading other books? Can we use it when we read in other subject areas?* We've surrounded a topic with four boxes whose headings help us organize details. We chose those headings based on our preview of the materials. This would be especially useful in history, science, music, or art.

Joe Louis: America's Fighter has now become a shared mentor book in this class. I can refer to it as we work on comprehension skills and strategies and writing techniques. It can become an anchor for us as we talk about periods in American history or the foibles of human nature. The 35 minutes we've spent with this mentor book will pay dividends in time saved as we move forward to new areas of study.

Trying it Out: An Invitation

Now is your chance to look through your favorite children's books and other sources for possible mentor texts. In addition to the questions posed in this chapter to evaluate a book's appropriateness as a read-aloud text, you can ask yourself the following questions to see if the book is worthy of becoming a mentor text in your classroom:

■ Does it provide clear examples of key aspects of good writing (e.g., the traits of good writing: ideas and details, organization, word choice, sentence fluency, voice, and conventions)?

■ Does the *content* encourage multiple connections?

Historical connections (e.g., biographies, time eras, famous events)

Background information for other required readings or subjects (e.g., *The Brain* by Seymour Simon to supplement the science textbook)

Clear examples of a genre or stylistic technique that will be used in guided reading or writing (e.g., memoir, point of view, organizational structures)

A dilemma or theme that will be explored in guided reading or independent reading (e.g., moral decision making in *The Summer My Father Was Ten* by Pat Brisson)

■ Can I use the book to focus on a specific teaching point in reading that will transfer to other texts across content areas?

■ Has it become a mentor book for me as a reader and a writer? Do I find myself thinking about lines from the book as I make connections between this book and my own reading and writing?

Finally, enjoy yourself. Let the natural actor or actress in you shine through. This is the moment in the whole apprenticeship model when we star as the mavens, the connectors, and the salespeople. It's up to us, through our knowledge and enthusiasm, to make these small changes in our presentation of new ideas and concepts, in our modeling, to make the literacy epidemic in our classrooms tip.

CHAPTER 3

Planning for Shared Practice

The air was charged with expectation. The children were studying "bubbleology." They were learning to use scientific methods of observation and note taking through experimentation with something very familiar: bubbles. For two days, the third graders in this after-school program had worked with two of my college students trying different commercially prepared bubble solutions and wands, making careful note of the quality of the resulting bubbles: how easily they formed and their size and duration. Today, they knew they would move outside to experiment with a new wand consisting of a long loop on a stick. If it worked well, the resulting bubbles would be the size of a Volkswagen. I had brought in the ingredients and recipe as well as a deep bucket. I told my college students how to make the bubble solution and pointed out the recipe. Then I left to check on the other groups of children working with my college students on other projects. When I returned to the bubbleology group, I found them outside and unable to form any bubbles with their new wand. The children and the college students looked dejected. When they walked through the steps they had taken to make the solution, I realized they hadn't measured the water. They'd simply poured in all the water I had brought. The resulting bubble solution was far too diluted to make bubbles of any size.

It wasn't their fault. I'd skipped a vital step in the teaching process. Simply telling or demonstrating is not sufficient when teaching a new skill, strategy, or procedure. The elementary and college students both needed shared and guided practice. They needed a chance to test their understanding by first telling me the steps as I prepared the solution (shared practice), and then an opportunity to do the work themselves with my guiding prompts (guided practice). My goal should not have been simply to get to the experiments as quickly as possible but to build the confidence and knowledge in doing hands-on science for both my preservice teachers and their after-school charges. The excitement that had been present until that time waned. The children lost interest in the experiments, and my preservice teachers questioned their ability to teach science.

Both the children and my college students became defensive, and my teaching role was more difficult because I hadn't spent the time up front in modeling or shared practice with them.

In this chapter, I explore that critical juncture in the apprenticeship model of learning—shared practice—when we begin to move from the teacher doing and the students watching to the students doing and the teacher watching. We are looking at the transfer of responsibility.

— Debbie

Using Shared Practice

Shared practice is the context in which students develop metacognition, the ability to think about their thinking so that they can be in control of their thinking. Marie Clay (1993b) addresses metacognition in her work with Reading Recovery as she focuses on the importance of students developing a "self-extending system." That system is one that helps students continue to grow as readers with each independent reading experience. It is a system that develops throughout our lives as we encounter new genres, new language structures, and new ways of thinking. For example, a beginning reader who has been relying on the language patterns and picture clues in predictable books ("I see Mommy painting. I see Mommy reading. I see Mommy sleeping.") discovers that not all books follow a pattern ("Number one monkey went over the bridge. Number two monkey went over the bridge. Number three and number four monkey went over."). As a reader develops a self-extending system, he or she takes that lesson and learns to have new expectations for his or her reading: Some books follow patterns faithfully throughout; others have a twist on that pattern.

Adult readers may be very proficient in reading in a particular genre, say historical fiction, but we have to use what we know to help us understand how to read in a new genre, such as the graphic novel *MAUS* about a concentration camp survivor. We don't necessarily need a teacher, if we are aware of our own thinking. What we need is a community in which we can explore the meaning of the text: a friend, a book group, or an online forum. What our developing readers need is the teacher and a supportive reading community. Shared practice provides both.

Shared practice gives us the opportunity to show students how specialists in a content area think and discuss. How do scientists approach a problem? How do musicians approach a new piece? What thinking patterns would a historian bring to the examination of a diary entry from 1944? What would a novelist notice while reading that diary entry? Shared practice can focus on the unique patterns of thought within a particular content area. It also allows us to focus on the reading process itself. Marie Clay (1993b) detailed the basic strategies that must be in place to develop this self-extending system. These strategies appear in Chapter 1, but we'll repeat them here:

- **Self-monitoring:** We constantly monitor our reading by asking, "Does this make sense?" "Does what I'm saying match the print?" "Does this sound like English?"

- **Cross-checking:** We further monitor our reading by asking those questions in conjunction with one another: "Does this make sense *and* look right?" "Does this look right *and* sound like English?" "Does this sound like English *and* make sense?"

- **Searching for more information**: If we run into a problem as we read, we have strategies to search for solutions. We can use our phonic knowledge to pronounce a word. We can use our knowledge of syntax and the meaning of the text to this point to predict the meaning of an unfamiliar word. We can read on, reread, ask someone, or google a term to get information if it isn't making sense.

- **Self-correcting:** We know how and when to self-correct to maintain efficient reading levels.

- **Fluency:** We read in phrases and sentences, not word by word. We use expressive reading coupled with appropriate speed so that our inner reading voice sounds like a radio broadcast or the audio track to a movie or documentary. We adjust our speed according to our purpose for reading. If we are reading a narrative, our reading pace picks up as we read a thrilling section. Our pace slows if we read about a tender moment. If we are reading expository text, we slow when we read unfamiliar or controversial ideas. We sail through familiar information. If we read aloud, our oral reading is a performance that allows others to share in the enjoyment of the text. We use phrasing and tonal qualities to make the reading more than a recitation of words, just as a pianist uses phrasing and tonal qualities to move from simply playing the notes to playing music.

As we teach our students to become avid readers across all subject areas, our big-picture view of the process can rest on these five strategies: teaching students to self-monitor, cross-check, search for information in order to problem-solve, self-correct efficiently, and read fluently. We are teaching these strategies while we teach the content of those subject areas, linking the strategies with the content. To ask, "Does this make sense?" in history class means, "Does this make sense with all that I know about this era?" To ask, "Does this make sense?" in math class means, "Does this sum correspond with the estimate I made?" Fluently reading a short story looks and sounds very different than fluently reading a science textbook. Marie Clay identified not only reading strategies but also thinking strategies that work across subject areas.

Shared practice is part of that critical transition between our modeling a new thought process and our students' independently applying that thought process. In shared practice, teachers are still doing the work but with students' conscious help. This help comes in the following stages:

1. Students *notice and name* what we are doing.

2. Students *predict* what we should do next.

3. Students *monitor* how well we did.

A Note From Debbie

Too often, because we teachers are so helpful, we inadvertently foster teacher dependence, rather than the independence found in a self-extending system. I have discovered some painful truths about myself over the years because some of my students have been so teacher-reliant.

Early in my career, I coached my high school's speech and debate teams. The debaters always wanted me to sit in the middle of the audience when they were in competition. I found out at the end of the first season that they were monitoring my reactions to the arguments. Apparently my eyebrows shot up when a debater made an assertion that put him or her on shaky ground, and this reaction warned the debater to make adjustments to this argument. The debaters weren't monitoring themselves; they were monitoring me and letting my reactions guide their decisions about what made sense or sounded right.

Those unintended cues are no different from my jumping in to correct a word as a child is reading aloud or taking a student's incorrect answer and reworking it to be correct. I once thought I was helping the child or protecting the child from classmates' ridicule. In essence, though, I was monitoring and correcting for my students. I wasn't teaching students how to be aware of those processes and do them on their own. In our teaching, we need to consciously move away from doing the thinking work for students rather than expecting them to try doing it on their own.

Apprenticeship Model Chart

MODELING	SHARED PRACTICE	GUIDED PRACTICE	INDEPENDENT PRACTICE
Teacher doing; Students watching	Teacher doing; Students helping	Students doing; Teacher helping	Students doing; Teacher watching

The role of shared practice in the apprenticeship model

These examples illustrate what shared practice looks like at different developmental levels.

Example 1:
Shared Practice in a Primary Classroom

Shared practice is familiar to most teachers at the primary level. It often takes the form of shared reading with the teacher handling a big book. Picture the following scene:

A kindergarten teacher sits next to a big book on an easel, surrounded by children sitting cross-legged on the floor. For days now, she has been pointing to the text as she reads, but today she asks the children to point to where she should start. Little fingers all point excitedly to the left side of the page. Students are *naming* through their gestures. The teacher puts the pointer under the first word in the line.

Then she asks students where she should go next when she reads. Arms sweep through the air: left to right. The students are *predicting* next steps based on what they understand about directionality. The teacher begins to read, pointing to each word, tracking left to right across the line.

When she finishes the page, she asks children to give her a thumbs-up or a thumbs-down to tell whether the pointer went across the line the way it should for good reading. They give the thumbs-up sign. Students are *monitoring* how well the teacher practiced reading from left to right across a line of print.

Students also benefit from the support of the rest of the group when its members provide answers. If a child is unsure, he or she can follow the lead of the other students in connection with the teacher's actions to modify or confirm his or her previous understanding of directionality in print.

Example 2:
Shared Practice in an Intermediate Classroom

In an intermediate classroom, shared practice is a natural spin-off from the modeling done during a read-aloud. Picture the students who have been introduced to *The Brain* by Seymour Simon. (Remember that in Debbie's sample lesson in Chapter 2, she focused on ways to remember new vocabulary and use visualizing and making connections as strategies to understand and remember conceptually dense information.) That teaching focus continues with new content-area vocabulary and information in mind. The teacher starts by asking students what the group could do to preview a new chapter in their science textbook and make connections to prior knowledge. The strategies they give (picture walk, looking at the table of contents, talking with a partner to share background knowledge) *name* the strategies. The teacher acknowledges all the good suggestions and then chooses to use a picture walk to look at the pictures and headings in the new chapter. Then, while reading a section, the teacher stops and asks what he could do to help him remember the new vocabulary. In this case, students are both *naming* and *predicting*. They offer their ideas: making an analogy, drawing a picture, acting out the word's meaning. The teacher acknowledges the possible strategies and proceeds with one of them, perhaps creating an analogy to help remember a new concept and then using repetition in the form of a group-made flash card to help connect the concept to the vocabulary word. At the end of the section, the teacher asks students to share responses with their study buddy as he poses the vocabulary words they identified in the reading. Students then *monitor* the effectiveness of the strategies to learn concepts and vocabulary based on their own responses and that of their study buddy.

Example 3:
Shared Practice in a Middle School Classroom

Shared practice can also be used in a middle school classroom. In a seventh-grade classroom, a teacher has been using short stories from the literature textbook to focus on literary elements and the writer's craft.

She sets the stage for Richard Connell's short story "The Most Dangerous Game." Today she is focusing on helping students notice words in the introduction that set the mood or the tone of a story. The teacher reads aloud the opening lines of the story:

"OFF THERE to the right—somewhere—is a large island," said Whitney. "It's rather a mystery—"

"What island is it?" Rainsford asked.

"The old charts call it 'Ship-Trap Island,'" Whitney replied. "A suggestive name, isn't it? Sailors have a curious dread of the place. I don't know why. Some superstition—"

On a projected copy of the story, the teacher uses a yellow pen to highlight *mystery*, *old charts*, *Ship-Trap Island*, *curious dread*, and *superstition*. She asks study buddies to buzz for a few minutes to note what she has done and to make a prediction as to why she's highlighted those particular words. The students are *noticing and naming* the strategy of highlighting words that evoke a mood.

Then the teacher confirms their observation. She asks students to *offer strategies* she might use to help her focus on the mood-invoking words. One student suggests using a graphic organizer, perhaps a map of the island to connect the words to the story. The teacher quickly draws and labels a picture of an island and lists the words on chart paper. She stops periodically as she continues to read aloud and asks students to help her identify "mood words." She adds those words to the list. Stopping a third of the way through the story, the teacher examines the list. She thinks aloud and asks for students' help in clustering the words and giving those clusters labels, such as "ominous," "eerie," and "inhuman."

At the end of the story, the teacher has the study buddies choose the word they think best captures the overall mood of the story. Each set of partners quickly shares its choice. Then she asks students to quickly rate the usefulness of the "list, group, label" strategy for their own understanding of the mood of the story, using a thumbs-up, thumbs in neutral position, or thumbs-down signal. In this way, students are *monitoring* the effectiveness of the method in helping them determine the mood. The teacher, in turn, is able to monitor the students' understanding of content through the set of words the partners suggest. By monitoring their acceptance of the reading strategy through their responses, she can do a quick assessment of both product and process.

What is the Tipping Point in Shared Practice?

In all three of the previous examples, teachers use the process of shared practice to help students become aware of and gain control of a new skill or strategy. They are "selling" literacy through their combined role of maven, connector, and salesperson. They have students hooked and interested, at least temporarily, in the subject.

The next goal is to make the message of literacy "sticky" so students are willing and able to do the reading work themselves. Again, *The Tipping Point* suggests three ways to "package" a message to make it "sticky":

1. Change the presentation to make it more practical and personal.

2. Use repetition strategically so the audience is actively involved with each repetition.

3. Encourage interaction through the message so the audience must do something.
(Gladwell, 2002, p.132)

Making the Presentation Practical and Personal

In early research about how to make *Sesame Street* successful, its developers videotaped children watching episodes of the shows. They noted when children looked at the screen and when they looked away. The researchers assumed children would look at the show when something new was presented or when something was confusing. They were wrong. Kids paid attention to the television when the sequence made sense to them. They looked away when the material was confusing. Consequently, the *Sesame Street* developers manipulated the presentation of material to make sure that children understood what they were supposed to attend to. By doing this, they increased the amount of time that the children looked at the screen. These adjustments made the "message" sticky by making it more practical and personal.

We can make our presentations more practical and personal by following the advice of Marie Clay (1993b) when we teach a new skill or strategy: We should teach that new skill or strategy using familiar material or simpler material. We can go back to the read-alouds that have captivated our students. We can use an article of local interest from a newspaper or magazine. We can write a simpler math problem, using the names of the children in the class as the characters in the story problem.

Using Repetition Strategically

The second way to make a message "sticky" is to use repetition. The developers involved with *Sesame Street* analyzed what happened as children watched a sequence multiple times. Their "aha!" moment came as they observed children watching James Earl Jones reciting the alphabet. The actor paused after each letter appeared on the screen. On the first viewing, children said the letter after the actor. After a couple of repetitions, children said the letter before Jones did. Finally, after enough repetitions, they would say the letter before it appeared on the screen. After that, the *Sesame Street* developers consciously used repetition in their shows, referring to it as "the James Earl Jones effect."

Mindless or purposeless repetition doesn't work though; we need repetition that engages children by allowing them to learn something with each repetition. As Gladwell writes, "Of course, kids don't always like repetition. Whatever they are watching has to be complex enough to allow, upon repeated exposure, for deeper and deeper levels of comprehension. At the same time, it can't be so complex that the first time around it baffles the children and turns them off." (Gladwell, 2002, p. 126)

We adults know the power of repetition to make a message "sticky." Most of us of a certain age can sing jingles from long-forgotten television commercials or the lyrics of once-popular songs. We originally found the music or the words catchy. Because we heard these commercials and songs so many times in our youth, we've found, often to our chagrin, that we remember them. This echoes what the *Sesame Street* researchers found: the children would reach a saturation point with repetitions ("Oh, no, not again!"). Then, after a break, they became nostalgic. They enjoyed chanting along, masters of the material.

I use an instructional method called "running reviews" to rehearse key vocabulary we've learned. I post an anchor chart in my classroom. Each time we learn a new word, I add it to the chart. We frequently review the list in one or two minutes by having study buddies tell each other what a word means or by giving an example of it in a sentence. Then I'll ask in what lesson we

A Note From Debbie

I can attest to the fact that my college students can sing the "Conjunction Junction" song from *Schoolhouse Rock*. Some can sing ditties naming the prepositions, and others can sing the list of the presidents of the United States. I find it interesting, though, that repetition is not enough to ensure understanding. After I did a review session on traditional grammar with my college students, one of them had a look of revelation on her face. I asked why. She sang a song of seemingly disconnected verbs, looked up at me, and said, "Are those the linking verbs?" They were. The repetition had helped my student remember the names of the linking verbs, but it had not given her the knowledge of why they were important.

As an aside, I'm very leery of programs based primarily on catchy songs and multiple repetitions. They promote memorization, not understanding. That is not the type of repetition we are advocating.

learned the target word, and students find themselves retelling Joe Louis's story or explaining how the brain works according to Seymour Simon.

We can capitalize on the power of repetition in our classrooms. We can use repetition and rehearsal to help our students learn new information. Then, after an interval, we need to come back to that information so students can show us that they are masters of it.

Repetition works when children are learning something with each repetition, but we have to be sure that what they are hearing makes sense. We're reminded of a cartoon from Gary Larson's *The Far Side*. The top half is titled "What we say to dogs." The owner is scolding his dog, saying, "OK, Ginger! I've had it! You stay out of the garbage! Understand, Ginger? Stay out of the garbage, or else!" The bottom half of the cartoon is labeled "What they hear." From Ginger's perspective, the owner is saying, "blah, blah, GINGER blah blah blah blah blah blah blah blah GINGER blah blah blah blah blah…"

What we say can sound like "blah, blah, blah" or it can make sense to our students. Sometimes we are in danger of overexplaining to the point that what we are saying does not make much sense to our students. When we coached children in Reading Recovery, we learned the utility of key directions, or prompts, using the same words in each repetition. We learned to choose our prompts based on the level of support the child needed at the time. Here's a sampling of prompts from Reading Recovery:

- "You try it!"
- "What can you try?"
- "Do you see a part that can help you?"
- "Sound the first part and think what would make sense."
- "Sound the first letter and think what would make sense."
- "Could it be _____?"

We learned more about the power of prompts as we read Peter Johnston's wonderful book *Choice Words*. The words we use with students are our most important tools as teachers. We must choose them carefully. While most of us have learned to use prompts as part of guided reading (which we explore in Chapter 4), we can also learn to use prompts as we talk through what we are doing as we model. We can encourage children to use specific language as they notice and name, predict, and explain during the shared practice portion of our lesson. The use of specific

Your Turn

What prompts do you use most frequently as you teach? Record yourself for 15 minutes as you have students help you in this shared practice phase of your teaching. Write down the words you use as you interact with students. Are you using specific language as you prompt or are you giving vague affirmations (e.g., "That's right" or "Good thinking")? Are you using the same prompts over and over, regardless of students' level of understanding? What would make your prompts more precise, more instructive, and more supportive in this shared practice phase of your teaching? What responses can you give to students so that they are using precise, specific language?

Now, as you plan for this shared practice phase in another lesson, jot down the prompts and comments you could use that (1) are positive in nature; (2) encourage students to notice, name, and predict; and (3) enhance student involvement.

language will help the child who, in independent reading, gets stuck and wonders what to do next. We hope, as our Reading Recovery teacher leader once said, the loudspeaker in the child's mind starts blaring our voice, saying something like, "Sound the first part and think what would make sense," or "What could you try?"

Encouraging Interaction

As the developers of *Sesame Street* found, a problem has to be complex enough to engage children's interest, yet easy enough for early success. Smith and Wilhelm's research (2002) with teen boys had similar findings. They posed the following question: Why are video games so engaging for teenage boys in particular? The boys themselves gave the answer. They need an engaging problem, early success, and social interaction. Video games offer an engaging problem. They start at an easy level, so the boys have early success. The players learn skills as they move up the levels of difficulty, and those skills will help them later with the more complex problems. The boys develop social networks that help each other by providing clues and "cheats." (Debbie can attest to answering late-night phone calls from friends of my teenage son seeking advice on how to conquer a particular level in a video game.) The boys use what they have learned. A response is required from them. They also have help along the way so that they don't become truly stuck.

Wilhelm and Smith found that the boys expect teachers to help them in similar ways, as part of the unwritten social contract of school. The boys, however, overwhelmingly share the perception that teachers break that social contract by showing how to do something and then assigning the work. The boys see the level of difficulty as too high without the social network there to provide help, which leaves them feeling discouraged. Reteaching or remediating doesn't make the message "sticky." It makes the message deadly. If only we would fulfill the unwritten social contract noted by Smith and Wilhelm's teen boys, we would not waste time fighting attitudes while we reteach. To fulfill that social contract, we must change our teaching to include shared practice. It is through shared practice that teachers provide the help students need and expect. This help must come long before students have tried and failed.

The hallmarks of a "sticky" message need to be observed: The message is personal and practical; it involves having the audience use repetition strategically, and the message is presented in such a way that the audience must actively respond. We'll save time in the long run if we spend adequate time with shared practice.

> *Your Turn*
>
> In what ways do you consciously fulfill the social contract described by the boys in Smith and Wilhelm's research?
> • Do you plan stopping points in the text for study buddies to share what they notice? What prompts will you use for students so that they interact and respond to each other with comments centered on the text?
> • Based on your teaching points, do you plan ways for students to interact with each other and with you as they predict what steps need to be taken next?
> • Again, based on your teaching points, what prompts will you use to help students monitor the effectiveness of the skill or strategy you are teaching?

Echoes Across Curricular Areas

You can use the shared practice time to buy instructional time by highlighting thinking processes used in all subject areas. During shared practice, students develop metacognition, the ability to think about and control their own thinking. They notice and name ways in which their teacher is thinking strategically, and then they practice those same patterns of thought. We can show students that the problem-solving strategies they are using in one subject area can help them in another. Look at the similarities between problem solving as readers, problem solving as mathematicians, and problem solving as musicians shown in the chart on page 78.

We help students make connections across content-area information, but we also help them make connections across ways of thinking. Through shared practice, we help students begin to think as readers, historians, musicians, mathematicians, artists, and scientists. We are teaching them ways to think about their thinking.

Change Over Time and Across Developmental Levels

Many years ago, Debbie had an opportunity to hear Ken Blanchard speak about his model for *The One Minute Manager* (1982). She was impressed with the situational nature of the prompts that good managers use with their workers. They praised and prompted differently, depending on the competence and commitment levels of each worker. Blanchard emphasized praising progress, even if the results weren't perfect, so that the worker would be encouraged rather than discouraged. He showed how managers needed to redirect a worker toward a goal if the results weren't yet perfect, and he emphasized using specific information in praising a worker, naming what the worker had accomplished.

In Reading Recovery, the situational level of our prompts is clear, echoing in many ways what Blanchard discovered as he worked in business. Look at the difference in the levels of these prompts by a primary teacher who is teaching directionality:

- (Pointing to the first word on the top line of the left page) "Should I start reading here?"

- (Pointing to the first word at the top of the page) "Should I start reading here or (pointing to the last word at the bottom of the page) should I start reading here?"

- (Pointing to the left-most word of the first line) "Should I start reading here or (pointing to the right-most word of the first line) should I start reading here?"

- (Covering everything on the page but the first line) "I want to look at the first word. Where in this line should I start?"

- (Showing the whole page) "Where should I start reading and which way should I go?"

The children are helping the teacher do the reading work, but the level of difficulty changes across those prompts. The first prompt gives them no choice but to pick the correct starting point. The prompts become progressively less specific until, with the last one in this sequence, students must understand directionality in order to "help" their teacher. If a child shows confusion by pointing out the wrong place in the text to start, the teacher knows that child needs more specific modeling and more supportive prompts.

If, however, a teacher constantly prompts with the most obvious clues so that the children are always correct, she is doing them a disservice. Students will become bored because they are not learning anything new, or they will become teacher-dependent, waiting for the adult to determine where to start reading on a page.

Let's revisit the middle school lesson for "The Most Dangerous Game" from earlier in the chapter (pages 71–72) to see how the prompts might differ in difficulty for older children. After the teacher reads the paragraph aloud, she projects a copy of the page and highlights the words *mystery*, *old charts*, *Ship-Trap Island*, *curious dread*, and *superstition*. She asks study buddies to buzz about what those words have in common. As the teacher eavesdrops on the quick discussions, she realizes that students aren't sure what she means. Some are looking to see what letters and sounds the words have in common, influenced perhaps by the class's previous study of sounds in poetry. Some pairs are assuming these will be spelling and/or vocabulary words. The prompt, "What do these have in common?" was too vague for students during this introductory lesson on mood.

The teacher quickly regroups. She acknowledges the students' good thinking in making connections to the poetry unit but refocuses their attention by giving a more specific prompt: "How is the author trying to make you feel by using these words? If this were a movie, what kind of movie would it be?" Students are successful in identifying the mood of the story with this prompt. Three or four stories from now, they will be ready to respond more confidently to the general prompt, "What do these words have in common?"

A Note From Debbie

A note of caution is needed here. Sometimes we assume a student understands the work and is simply not applying himself, when he truly doesn't understand what we are asking. My teaching experience was primarily with upper elementary and middle school children, until I took the opportunity to work with first graders through Reading Recovery.

During my first day with Karrington, I assessed his knowledge of sounds and letters. The only letters he could name were the ones in his first name. I made a note that Karrington recognized *a, i, o, g, k, n, r,* and *t.* Thank goodness he had a long first name, was my mental note. On day two, I showed Karrington a very simple pattern book with clear pictures. We did a picture walk through the book, using much of the language of the text: "This is a table." "This is a chair." So far, so good. Then I started reading the book to Karrington. When I pointed to the word *a* in the text, I said in my most encouraging voice, "You can read that word, Karrington. It's the same as a letter in your name." He looked at me blankly. Instead of changing my prompt, I started badgering him. "I know you know that word, Karrington. You told me its name yesterday." Finally in frustration, Karrington said, "Honest to God, Mrs. Corpus, I've never seen that before in my life!" I looked down and suddenly realized that the representation of *a* in this text was nothing like the representation Karringon was familiar with. I was looking at the information through an adult's eyes, not those of a new learner.

a a

WHAT A READING TEACHER SAYS	WHAT A MATH TEACHER SAYS	WHAT A MUSIC TEACHER SAYS
Preview the text. What is it likely to be about?	Preview the section in textbook. What is it asking you to learn? What will the problems ask you to do?	Preview the music. What type is this?
Identify the main idea and the details as you read.	Identify the key information in the story problem and eliminate unnecessary details.	Will it be fast or slow? What key is it in?
Visualize what is happening in the story and use the clues in the text to predict what will happen next.	Visualize the question the story problem is setting up for you. Use clues in the problem to estimate the answer.	Listen in your mind as you scan the music. Use clues to predict how the melody and accompaniment will probably sound.
Ask if your prediction makes sense with all that you know from your background information.	Ask if your estimate makes sense with all that you know about how numbers work.	Ask if your prediction makes sense with all that you know about the composer and the type of music you are studying.
Read on to see if your prediction is confirmed or disproved. If your prediction was wrong, reread to see what clues misled you.	Work the problem to see if the answer you get is close to your estimate. If not, figure out what went wrong in your thinking.	Play through the music to see if it matches what you heard in your mind. If not, figure out which clues misled you.
Work on the sequence of events in the story.	Work out the sequence in which you must work through the problem.	Find natural breaking points in the music and work on the sections.
Give the word a temporary pronunciation. Come back to it at the end of the sentence or paragraph to see if you can figure it out then.	Guess and check.	Play the melody line first. Then come back and put both hands together.
Think of a story or movie that is structured like this or has a character like this to help you with this more complex story.	Work a simpler problem to help you figure out a formula for the more complex problem.	Review a simpler piece that uses this same technique.
Use a story map or some other graphic organizer to help you understand the structure of the story.	Draw a picture to understand what the problem is asking.	Listen to someone else play this so you know what it is supposed to sound like.
Use fix-up strategies if what you read doesn't make sense, sound right, or look right.	Use fix-up strategies if the answer you get doesn't make sense, sound right, or look right.	Use fix-up strategies if the music doesn't make sense overall, sound right, or match up with the written notes.

Problem-solving similarities among reading, math, and music

Students actively engaged in shared practice lesson

Possible Solutions to Management and Behavioral Issues

In *The One Minute Manager,* Blanchard also talked about ways to handle work that wasn't going well. His first point was to never punish or reprimand learners, because that would immobilize them. The manager had to focus on what the learners needed and then redirect them. If, however, a worker was not performing a familiar task well, Blanchard suggested a one-minute reprimand focusing specifically on the work, not the person. The reprimand needed to be immediate and followed with an affirmation that the manager knew the worker could do the work. The purpose was to get the worker back on track toward a goal, not to devalue the person.

Following Blanchard's lead, we can assess our own use of the prompts we use during shared practice as follows:

1. Are we clear in our goals and in what we are teaching?

- Have we moved beyond the general "I'm teaching this story" or "I'm teaching Chapter 7" to an identification of our teaching points?

- Have we thought through how Marie Clay's reading strategies are translated into thinking strategies in the specific content areas?

- Have we been clear in our modeling and in our explanation of those strategies?

2. Do we prompt and praise immediately?

- Are we specific?

- Do we praise approximations toward the goal?

3. Do we avoid criticizing students as they make their first approximations?

- Do we affirm our belief in the abilities of our students, even if we have to correct them?

To Sum it Up

We save time by taking the time to plan for the shared-practice aspect of our teaching. We think carefully of the words we use and the target of those words.

In essence, we move from modeling and demonstration to shared practice by having students notice and name the targeted action, predict the next steps, and monitor our success. We are still *doing* while the students are *helping*.

We save time in shared practice by doing the following:

- Focusing our message on big-picture reading strategies that cross disciplines: self-monitoring, cross-checking, searching, self-correcting, and fluency

- Making the message of literacy "sticky" by making it personal and practical, using repetition, and requiring a student response

- Avoiding the discouragement and resistance that come from failure, reteaching, and remediation

If we plan for shared practice, we help the students experience success. Used thoughtfully, our guiding words have amazing power.

A Closer Look at Shared Practice

In Chapter 3, we've explored the phase of the apprenticeship model in which the focus has shifted from the teacher demonstrating and explaining to the phase in which students are helping the teacher perform the new skill or strategy—shared practice. Students are actually rehearsing the new skill or strategy in a low-risk situation with immediate correction or clarification available from either the teacher or from the other children. Students notice and name the steps in the new skill or strategy, then they predict which steps come next. As the teacher continues with this aided demonstration, students monitor the effectiveness of the strategy or skill: Did the teacher do it correctly? Did it work? What changes were needed?

Throughout this phase, the teacher moves back and forth between being under the complete guidance of students to doing all the work and explanation if students are stumped. The teacher is constantly making decisions about how much support students need. Should he or she follow an incorrect direction from students to show what could happen, should he or she clarify the misunderstanding through his or her choice of prompts, or should he or she repeat the correct demonstration without student assistance?

In Chapter 3, we applied concepts from *The Tipping Point* to this phase in the apprenticeship model.

- We looked at ways to make shared practice practical and personal by using simple or familiar materials.

- We examined ways to use repetition effectively, making certain students learn or affirm a concept with each repetition.

- We learned that to make a message "sticky" we must involve students in *doing* something, interacting and responding as they practice the new skill or strategy.

This follow-up contains an outline for a successful lesson Debbie has used in intermediate and middle school classrooms that moves from modeling to shared practice to the beginnings of guided practice. The shifts from modeling to shared practice aren't clear-cut or linear. The apprenticeship model allows the teacher to move back to modeling as well as to advance to more guidance from students depending on their needs. See if you can also find the elements that potentially make the message "sticky" and therefore memorable.

Sample for an Intermediate or Middle School Classroom: *National Geographic Explorer*

This is a lesson I (Debbie) have taught to various grade levels. The specifics for this lesson plan come from teaching it in a third-grade classroom at Ann's school. Ann had already worked with the group on how to figure out new words. As students shared what they had learned with Ann, they referred to an anchor chart that she had constructed with them. As I looked around the classroom, it was obvious that Ann's students were interested in many things. I could see motorcycle books, puzzle books, and a variety of chapter books tucked by student desks for independent reading. I also observed that students already had routines in place so that they could work quietly in small groups, without a teacher constantly monitoring them. These observations helped me to quickly tailor my basic plan to Ann's class. (Again, once you've identified your teaching points for a lesson, you can look at your mentor texts for the best one to use or revisit as you complete your planning frame.)

Mentor Text: *National Geographic Explorer*

Key teaching point for reading: Authors often use interesting details to hook readers, so readers need to sort out what is important from what is simply interesting. They use their purpose for reading to determine what is important to remember. Readers actively work to identify main ideas for their purpose and then focus their memory on those ideas.

Content connections: Other than in textbooks, we find expository text most often in periodicals and newspapers, particularly in the areas of science, health, history, and current events. Students often read current events in magazines at school, such as *Time for Kids, The Weekly Reader,* and *National Geographic Explorer.* As they read, students must discern what is important and what is added to make the article attractive or memorable. They must decide what information to remember and how to remember it.

- *Science:* Writers often use a new discovery or an unanswered question to hook the reader's interest. "Global Warming Will Cause the Arctic to Melt by 2050" or "How Green is He?" for example, are titles of science articles focusing on global warming. Readers must sort out what is fact from what is opinion in these articles. They must also look at the qualifications and the purposes of the author.

- *Health:* Articles on health are often headlined in ways to touch students' own personal worries: "Riding Your Bicycle May be Dangerous to Your Health" or "Over 30 Percent of School-Aged Children are Obese." Students are drawn to these articles based on their own interests or perceptions of themselves. Again, all readers need to sort out what is fact, what is important to remember, and what is interesting but not important to remember.

- *Social Studies:* Ongoing coverage of national or international current events may seem unimportant to students who do not have a direct personal connection to the topic of a war or the economy or events in a far-off country. Readers need to know how to set a purpose for themselves and how to use interesting details to maintain their interest, while remembering information that may come under the category of "boring but important."

Lesson Plan Outline

Management: Students sit with a partner. Each pair has a pencil or marker. I have multiple copies of the same issue of *National Geographic Explorer,* so every pair has a copy. I limit resources in this way to encourage partners to work together. Additional back issues of the magazine are available so that partners have some choice in the issue they'll examine in the follow-up activity. I have copies of a chart I'll give students to complete at their desks after we work together on a display copy of it.

Before beginning the lesson, students practice responding to the signal I will use to get their attention if I need to shift their attention to work with the whole class. I have them tell each other their favorite dessert, and then in 30 seconds or so I raise my hand and say, "May I have your attention, please?" The students are to stop talking and raise their hand as a signal to those who didn't hear me. I praise students for their prompt response and then have them practice again by asking them to tell each other the name of their favorite movie or television show. Again, after 30 seconds I ask for their attention. If a pair simply puts up their hands and continues talking, I point out that they've fulfilled only half the expectation and kept the classroom from becoming quiet. If necessary, we practice getting quiet and shifting attention one more time.

Setting a Purpose: I empty a canvas bag filled with popular magazines, such as *People, Ladies Home Journal, Camping, The Smithsonian, The Week, Time, Popular Mechanics, Astronomy.* I hold up a *Ladies Home Journal* with a pink background and a prominent picture of a mouthwatering chocolate cake. The title of the featured article is in bold letters: "Walk Off Ten Pounds in Ten Days" or something along those lines. I explain that I was initially drawn to the magazine because of its promise of easy weight loss, but I was enticed to buy it because of that tempting picture of chocolate cake. Then I show *Camping* magazine and read the headline that attracts me and explain why: "There's an article on the Boundary Waters, an area where my family has camped in the past. I wonder if the authors will talk about places I've been before." I pull out another magazine and have students make predictions about what would entice a person like me to buy it. We do this with two more magazines. This helps us come to the conclusion that magazine publishers use some kind of detail to hook our interest and make us want to buy the magazine.

I tell students that authors do the same thing. Sometimes they use an interesting detail to hook our interest so we'll read, but we have to be careful or we may miss the main point of the article. I use an example from a local radio show, *One Minute of Science*: "In one minute, the radio hosts hook us with a strange but true fact, and then they go into depth to tell us something important about the scientific phenomena. As listeners and readers, we need to be able sort out the main message from the hook. Today we'll find ways to distinguish between important ideas and inter-esting details. In fact, we'll use what we learn from our reading today to do our own *One Minute of Science* radio show."

✔ BEFORE READING

I model this process using an article about penguins from *National Geographic Explorer.* First we look over the whole article, and I read only the headings. Then we predict what the text will mainly be about, based on those headings and connections to information we already know about penguins. Students are filled with information based on the movie *March of the Penguins.* I chart their predictions about the gist of the article.

Then I model using my own knowledge to determine a purpose for reading the article. Because I'll use the penguin article to develop my own *One Minute of Science* show, I need both important information and one or two interesting details to hook an audience.

✔ DURING READING

With that purpose in mind, I read the first section of the article aloud, stopping to do a think-aloud as I go. I have a display chart ready to complete with the following three sections: Important Ideas; Interesting Facts; Important, Interesting, or Unfamiliar Words. When I finish reading the first section, I write the key ideas, interesting facts, and key vocabulary on the chart. I invite students to debrief: What did I do? (noticing and naming), What would I probably do next? (predicting), How well did I do in picking out what was important and any interesting details in preparation for sharing the information in a one-minute radio program? (monitoring).

Through this section, I've moved from modeling and demonstration in the apprenticeship model to the brink of shared practice. Next, I'm going to share the practice with students by having them tell me how to chart key ideas, interesting facts, and key vocabulary.

Now I distribute the copies of *National Geographic Explorer* and blank copies of the chart to students, and I read the next section to them, stopping often so partners can talk about what is important and what is interesting and jot down ideas on their chart. Then I share what I consider important and why. I ask for a thumbs-up sign if students agree. After I ask for other possibilities from students and their reasons for suggesting them, I validate their approximations. Based on student responses, I add all or some of the ideas to the chart.

I read the next section aloud, again stopping for partners to talk and jot their ideas on their chart. Then I ask volunteers to tell me what I should record based on what they found important or interesting. I ask for a thumbs-up from those who agree. Again, I validate and encourage approximations. I add those facts, details, and vocabulary to the class chart. At this point, I am using shared practice with my students, testing their ideas on me.

However, I want to move away from teacher dependence and have my students help one another. I combine two pairs to make a foursome and assign the following roles: leader, note taker, decider, and observer. The small group's job is to work together on the next sections, determining importance, identifying interesting details, and noting vocabulary. The leader takes charge of the group's work, determining how the group will read each section (e.g., silently to themselves or aloud by a designated reader). He or she also poses the questions to get the chart completed. The note taker is in charge of writing on the group's chart. The decider has the final word if the group has a disagreement about what to put on the chart. The observer's job is to keep the group on track and to monitor: Does everyone understand the section? Did the group find at least one important fact in the section? In this portion of the lesson, students are sharing the practice with one another, coaching and correcting misunderstandings as needed.

✔ AFTER READING

When the small groups are finished, I call for volunteers to help me complete the class chart. Then I model preparing an impromptu *One Minute of Science* presentation: I circle an interesting detail that will be my hook, put a check next to the main ideas that I think are most important, number them in the order I think would make sense to present to a listening audience, and write a sentence summarizing the main idea of the whole article to use as my closing statement. Then I perform my *One Minute of Science* in my best radio-announcer voice.

A follow-up I did in this class was to let students choose another issue of *Explorer* to read in their foursome. Each group worked through an article, made a chart, and then did its own version of *One Minute of Science*. The students provided guidance for each other as I moved from group to group, coaching. While none of the performances was stellar, we certainly could celebrate the approximations. As with most lessons focusing primarily on shared practice moving toward guided practice, one experience is not enough to make the message truly stick.

Echoes: Debriefing Process and Content

Throughout this lesson, I monitored how students categorized facts into main ideas and interesting details. I also monitored that students understood what the article was saying about penguins. The *One Minute of Science* follow-up, along with the individual charts of important ideas, interesting details, and vocabulary allowed me to assess the success of the lesson. Like an athletic coach, I see no benefit to grading practice. I need to assess students to see what they learned and what else they need to know. I use my observations and the evidence to determine what's next in lesson planning. In this lesson, I could see that students needed additional practice in this type of reading material to satisfy me that they were using their purpose to identify main ideas and interesting details and to connect them in their presentations.

Your Turn

Regarding the tipping point in shared practice:
• In what ways did Debbie act as a salesperson, a maven, or a connector in order to "sell" the lesson?
• What did Debbie build into the lesson to make it "sticky"?
Regarding the apprenticeship model:
• In what portions of the lesson was Debbie modeling and demonstrating?
• In what portions did Debbie move to having the students share in the practice?

Trying it Out: An Invitation

Look at a lesson plan you've developed in which you know you did an effective job both modeling a reading strategy and hooking students' interest in the topic. Perhaps you are particularly pleased with the think-aloud you did during a read-aloud session or during the sinking/floating demonstration that really got students interested in reading their science text. Whatever it was, give yourself credit for your work as a salesperson, maven, and connector.

Now examine the shared practice portion of that lesson.

- In what ways were your students noticing and naming what you were doing?

- Were they able to predict what you needed to do next as a strategic reader and thinker?

- What invitations did you give them to assess the effectiveness of the skill or strategy you were teaching?

Draw a line down the center of a piece of theme paper. On the left, jot down what you did well in each of those areas. On the right, brainstorm ways to strengthen those aspects of shared practice. As you work, consider how you might make your presentation even more practical and personal.

- Did you use familiar material, or is there something you could use that would be even more accessible?

- Did you use simpler material so your teaching point was not lost in the complexity of the text? If not, what simpler materials would work for both the content and the reading strategy?

- Did you build in meaningful repetition? If not, in what ways could you build in "running reviews" to remind students of what they have learned?

- Is there a way to revisit ideas using the precise language of well-formed prompts? What might those prompts be?

- In this shared practice portion, did you call on students to *do* something, to interact in some way? If not, what could you add to your plan to get students to actively respond?

- Finally, in what ways were you gathering information about the students' grasp of both the content knowledge and the reading strategy being taught? What adjustments could you make in subsequent lessons to strengthen both the product and the process?

After you've analyzed one of your lessons and found ways to focus more on effective shared practice in your planning, you can now focus on shared practice in your teaching. Consciously focus on having students notice and name what you are doing during a demonstration. Have them predict what you should do next. Have them assess how well you employed the skill or strategy. At the end of each day, jot down your successes in the use of shared practice. Celebrate your approximations and your successes.

CHAPTER 4

Planning for Guided Practice

My older brother, Paul, somehow made it all the way to sixth grade without learning to read beyond a first-grade level. At the time, teachers just didn't know how to deal with older nonreaders. The easiest solution was to send struggling readers in upper grades to the first-grade classroom for their reading instruction—obviously, not the best solution. This situation prompted my parents to look for a private tutor for Paul. My mother was given the name of a retired teacher, Miss Hoyt, who proved to be the key to my brother's success in becoming literate.

Miss Hoyt was a no-nonsense person. She told my mother before Paul's first session that she wasn't sure she could help him and that she wouldn't "waste my time, his time, or your money" if she could not. Her tone changed completely by the end of that first session, and she stated she thought she could help.

I've asked my brother what Miss Hoyt did during these sessions. He said that she let him choose the book he wanted to read. While he read, she would sit across the room and correct and encourage him from there. Miss Hoyt taught Paul how to use the sounds of letters and words that he struggled with in the text. After a year of sessions, my brother had made remarkable progress, reading well above the sixth-grade level! In the last session, Paul said he looked up at Miss Hoyt after reading that day's text and tears were streaming down her face.

In many ways, Miss Hoyt was way ahead of her time. By sitting across the room, she was minimizing the tendency to jump in too soon to help, thus, maximizing Paul's independence in problem solving. Using the instructional techniques we now use in guided practice, Miss Hoyt supported my brother's learning by correcting and encouraging him; yet she let him do the thinking and the problem solving, helping only when he needed it. She also gave Paul a choice in what he read, suggesting that he bring a book that would interest him. Finally, Miss Hoyt knew the importance of bonding with her student and believing in his potential to become literate.

Paul found school a lot easier after Miss Hoyt. He went on to college and later became a successful businessman. In his words, "Some people have a big impact on your life . . . little Miss Hoyt certainly did on mine." My brother's testimony is an enviable legacy for any teacher.

— Ann

Observing my brother's struggles as a reader and the success he found under Miss Hoyt's guidance had an impact on me as well. I wanted to be a teacher, and I wanted to be like Miss Hoyt. However, early in my career I learned that teaching reading is not easy! I soon discovered the frustration of working with a student or group of students who struggle to read and having no idea how to help. Often, these students would try very hard, but they would get confused, make errors, and eventually get so discouraged that they would give up. I would sit by, observing their struggle and making desperate but futile attempts to help, without understanding what was causing the problem or how to effectively intervene. A nightmare for both my students and me! Training as a Reading Recovery teacher was my way out of this nightmare. Through Reading Recovery, the early intervention program designed by Marie Clay, I learned how to listen analytically to students' oral reading and responses to text in order to discern why students made errors and guide their thinking using carefully chosen language that prompted them to do the thinking and problem solving as they read. With this guidance and support, my students became more strategic and successful. These interactions with students increased my knowledge of what they already knew about reading, what they needed to learn next to continue developing as readers, and what level of text would provide that critical balance between practicing the strategies and skills they did control and effectively dealing with new challenges.

One of the biggest challenges we face as teachers of grades 3–8 is meeting the diverse needs of the students in our classrooms. Reading is a skill basic to learning—whether in English/language arts, math, social studies, or science. However, the students in any classroom have a range of reading levels, capabilities, and instructional needs. We may have students who are reading two or three grade levels below their current grade level, yet who have a deep and rich base of background knowledge. There may be students who stumble over every tenth word in a text. Some students may read like movie stars reciting their lines, but as we listen to and work with them we realize they are very good at calling words but have no clue about what they have read. We may have students who are stuck in a genre. They read the books of Brian Jacques and remember every creature and action, but they look blankly at a page in their science textbook. We also may have students who read above grade level but still need guidance and instruction to hone and improve their thinking and response to what they read. When it comes right down to it, every student in a classroom is at a unique place along a very wide continuum of literacy development. How can teachers discern and meet the needs of all these individuals in a classroom? And how can teachers who teach multiple sections within a content area meet the literacy needs of the 150 students they might teach each day?

In this chapter, I explore guided practice, the important stage in the apprenticeship model when students are doing the reading and thinking while the teacher assumes the role of keen observer who intervenes only when necessary to assist students' effective processing of text. Through guided practice, teachers are able to address the strengths and needs of individual students. With this guidance, students reach the cusp of becoming independent and self-extending readers.

What is Guided Practice?

Shared practice in reading generally engages whole or large groups and, as we said in Chapter 3, provides that transition in teaching and learning between our modeling the thinking readers do and the independent application of this thinking by students. Guided practice is the natural extension of shared practice, in which teachers begin to shift a greater amount of the responsibility for reading and thinking onto students. Guided practice works best through small-group work with students who have similar instructional needs. One group might need to learn how to use the features of nonfiction text in order to understand the content. Another group might need to work on reading multisyllable words and using context to predict the meaning of these words. Still another group might need to work on how to keep track of characters in a story and determine how each affects what happens as the story unfolds. By grouping students according to their instructional strengths and needs and by appropriately adjusting the size of the group and the amount of instructional time, we can focus on the particular skills and strategies the students within these groups require.

Apprenticeship Model Chart

MODELING	SHARED PRACTICE	GUIDED PRACTICE	INDEPENDENT PRACTICE
Teacher doing; Students watching	Teacher doing; Student helping	Student doing; Teacher helping	Students doing; Teacher watching

The role of guided practice in the apprenticeship model

In the small-group context of guided practice, the teacher engages students in conversation about the thinking and problem solving readers do in order to comprehend a particular text. Students are encouraged to try on this thinking and apply the skills and strategies they are learning as they read the text—all with the observant support of the teacher. Having knowledge of what our students already have under control in reading allows us to build from there: we can help students to use what they know and prompt their thinking to meet new challenges.

The Zone of Proximal Development and Guided Practice

If we stop and think about how we learn something new, we realize that we rely on the modeling, explanation, and support of more knowledgeable others. In Chapter 1, we discussed Vygotsky's Zone of Proximal Development, or ZPD (see pages 14–15). As you recall, Soviet psychologist Lev Vygotsky emphasized the importance of this social context for teaching and learning. According to Vygotsky, the teacher and student working together establish an instructional context in which the teacher supports and guides the student in doing something he or she could not learn to do without this support. This is what Vygotsky called the Zone of Proximal Development.

Learning within the ZPD is mediated through language and communication. As the teacher talks with the student, prompting him or her to think strategically and to problem solve new challenges, the student eventually internalizes that language and learns to talk himself or herself through challenging parts of a text. During the process, the teacher is constantly making decisions about what the student can do and what kind of support is needed to extend the student's learning.

Vygotsky theorized that it is more than the teacher teaching and the student learning; rather, the teacher and student both contribute to what happens as they talk and interact. The flow of learning and assistance is not one-way, i.e., from teacher to learner. Barbara Rogoff, an expert in Vygotskian theory, explains:

> *"The effectiveness of adults in structuring situations for children's learning is matched by children's eagerness and involvement in managing their own learning experiences. Children put themselves in a position to observe what is going on; they involve themselves in the ongoing activity; they influence the activities in which they participate; and they demand some involvement with the adults who serve as their guides. . . . Together, children and adults choose learning situations and calibrate the child's level of participation so that the child is comfortably challenged.*
> [Rogoff (1986), p. 38]

Your Turn

How can you make the most of the give and take between you and your students?

• Do you jot down notes as you observe individual students during a lesson and discuss your observations with each student later on?

• Do you ask students about what they do well as a reader? What they find difficult?

• Do you encourage students to give you feedback about what they have learned or what still confuses them?

The give and take between teacher and students is what makes guided practice both powerful and fulfilling.

I recall working with Sam, a fourth grader who was reading more than a year below grade level. Sam was very perceptive and particularly able to express his needs and frustrations as a learner. After listening to him read a page of text where he stumbled over every word that was more than two syllables, I suggested that the big words in the text were difficult for him. I knew Sam had the background experience to understand what was going on in the story, so I suggested that he do two things as he reread this passage. First, he should use what he knew about how people act to understand the situation in the story. Secondly, I chose a couple of the multisyllable words Sam had struggled with and showed him on a whiteboard how to take the word apart—noticing parts of the word that were familiar to him and reading across the word in chunks, rather than letter by letter.

After watching me demonstrate this process on a couple of words, Sam was able to see how to take other words apart that had challenged him initially. He candidly declared, "No one ever showed me how to do that. My second-grade teacher used to always yell at me and tell me to sound the words out, but I couldn't! This is much easier!" Sam was right on—it is easier to look for the patterns of letters and sounds within words. Brain research supports this, and this is why we should not say to students, "Sound it out." Children take the "sound it out" prompt literally, sounding letter by letter. What we really want to encourage is using patterns of letters in the English language to "chunk" the sounds. I encouraged Sam to reread the passage, thinking about the story and using the word-solving strategy he had just learned on any words that were difficult for him. He went away from this lesson with a new strategy for solving tricky words and a renewed sense of his ability as a reader. I, in turn, had a better understanding of Sam as a learner and of how to proceed with guiding his reading.

Working Within the ZPD in Guided Practice

Our goal for instruction in guided practice is for our students to become independent, self-extending learners who are able to find solutions for the challenges in text on their own. We take care to set an appropriate task for our students, knowing what they know and what they are ready to learn at this point in their development. We choose a text that is at a suitable level and that provides opportunities for working on the strategies and skills students need. As students encounter challenges in the text, we calibrate our support to ensure that *they* are doing the thinking and problem solving. We judiciously step in to prompt or ask questions only when they need our assistance. We design our prompts and questions to promote, not preempt, students' thinking. What teachers say to students, and how they say it, has a direct effect on what students learn.

Language in guided practice is a teaching tool—it is through our conversation with students that we model and mediate their thinking as they process text. Language also provides a means for assessing learning—how students respond gives teachers a window into their thinking processes.

A Note From Ann

A word of caution about oral reading during a guided reading lesson: Oral reading has been described as a "foggy window" through which the teacher observes students as they process text. When students read aloud, teachers can observe their behaviors and listen to their reading, i.e., repetitions, pauses, multiple attempts at words, self-corrections, and spontaneous remarks they may make as they strive to get the author's message. However, because the brain is so complex and thinking is not observable, teachers can only draw hypothetical conclusions about what the student is and is not doing. Certainly, the more a teacher works with a student, the better he or she will become at understanding how that student processes text and how to support the student's growth as a reader. In addition, research tells us that different parts of the brain are activated during oral and silent reading. During oral reading, the speech and language center of the brain is activated, which makes sense, because the student is using speech to read the text aloud. During silent reading, the cognitive center of the brain is the most active. This difference should be taken into consideration when analyzing and hypothesizing about students' thinking while reading. Finally, if a student is having significant difficulty understanding a text, it could be that the text is too difficult. If the student doesn't understand vocabulary, is unfamiliar with syntax, and is making errors on more than 10% of the words on a page, this indicates that the book is too hard.

When a book is too difficult, one avenue is to abandon it and choose an easier text that meets the same objectives. This is often a way to build background knowledge that equips a student to then go back and read more difficult books successfully. Another option is to use the text for shared reading and model for students the thinking and problem solving needed to understand the text. Sometimes, just spending time building background, using graphic organizers to make connections, and focusing on key vocabulary to support students' understanding and processing before returning to the text are enough to get them back on track.

Three Key Information Systems in Text

Guided practice involves continuing the development of those basic strategies we've mentioned in earlier chapters: self-monitoring, cross-checking, searching for information, self-correcting, and fluency. The prompts we use strategically direct students to use three key information systems in text—meaning, language structure, and graphophonics—in an *integrated* way to read with understanding, fluency, and accuracy. Each of these systems connects with the others. In order to make sense of what we are reading, we must use our understanding of how language works and accurately read the text.

Let's take a closer look at each of these information systems. It's important to have a clear understanding of what each of these cue systems involve in order to make on-the-spot decisions during guided practice to prompt students to access and integrate the information from these systems.

Meaning

The purpose of reading is to get the author's message. Effective readers are always asking, *Does this make sense?* All instruction should be based on this assumption and directed toward developing students' understanding of what they read. Readers use their life experience, knowledge of the world, and understanding of how books work to construct meaning as they read. Thanks in large part to the work of Keene and Zimmerman (1997), we know that comprehension can actually be *taught* by focusing on the thinking strategies used to understand text, and not just *assessed*, as we did in the old days, with questions after a student reads. These strategies are:

Making connections: using prior knowledge and experience to connect with the text—making text-to-self, text-to-text, and text-to-world connections—both to better understand and to compare/contrast what is known and experienced versus what the author says

Determining importance: distinguishing what's important for the story or topic from what's perhaps interesting or less important

Asking questions: asking questions of the author while reading the text to focus on and better understand the story or information presented

Visualizing: creating sensory images—visual, auditory, olfactory, tactile, and taste—to relate to and deepen understanding of text

Making inferences: combining prior knowledge and experience with information in the text to make predictions, draw conclusions, and personally interpret the text

Retelling or synthesizing: thinking about what's most important to integrate the ideas and information in the text to determine the author's purpose and message

Self-monitoring and fixing it up: when comprehension breaks down, using all information in a text—meaning, language structure, and graphophonic—to get back on track to maintain understanding

As we discussed in Chapters 2 and 3, the foundation for the cognitive strategies for comprehension forms during read-aloud and shared practice with the teacher modeling how readers think before, during, and after reading a text. By thinking aloud, the teacher externalizes what goes on in the mind while one reads and supports students in taking on the thinking strategies they use to understand what they read. Readers do not use these cognitive strategies in a mutually exclusive way; the strategies overlap. Readers use a combination of the strategies to deepen and modify their understanding, to resolve confusion, to analyze and evaluate new concepts, and to grow as thinkers and readers. It is during guided practice that teachers can encourage and support students' use of these strategies. The teacher guides the students to do the thinking that is most helpful in constructing meaning and resolving conceptual problems as they read.

Language Structure

Syntax, the way in which words are put together to form phrases, clauses, or sentences, is the "glue" in text, connecting individual words (decoding) and meaning (comprehension). Syntax allows us to predict words and overall meaning as we read. Syntax allows us to confirm that what we have read is correct, on both the word level and the meaning level.

Each language has its own syntax, or language structure. For example:

- In English, adjectives usually come before the noun they modify. In many other languages, the adjectives follow the noun.

- In English, the order of words in a sentence determines their function (e.g., "The dog bit the man" has a very different meaning than "The man bit the dog."). Yet in a number of other languages, the word order is unimportant because the grammatical function of a word is determined by its ending. (All you former Latin scholars, think of the five declensions for masculine nouns.)

- In English, questions are often formed by inverting the normal positions of the subject and verb (e.g., "The man is hurt" becomes "Is the man hurt?"). We use a specific mark of punctuation to indicate a question, and that mark is at the end of the sentence. The word order of the sentence signals a question long before we reach the question mark. In Spanish, an inverted question mark at the start of a sentence alerts readers that a question is being asked, and it's further confirmed by a question mark at the end of the sentence.

- Speakers of English dialects follow specific grammatical rules. In some dialects, the third-person-singular present-tense verb has disappeared. So instead of saying, "He walks to the store," a speaker in that dialect would say, "He walk to the store." In the same way, the verb form "to be" has completely vanished from some dialects. Instead of standard English's awkward changes for the infinitive *to be* (I *am* here. You *are* here. He *is* here.), some dialects simply use the infinitive form (I *be* here. You *be* here. He *be* here.).

Students bring with them the knowledge of how the English language works in their everyday lives in their own dialects or in the transformation of their home language to English. To check this syntactic system, readers ask themselves, *Does this sound right? Does it sound like something I would say?*

The language of books, however, often differs from spoken language. A child may see "I don't have a pencil" in print and may read, "I ain't got no pencil" because that is what *sounds* right. This is not a decoding error. It is a syntactic error. Most readers will mentally transform sentences to match their own sense of grammatical structures. They'll stop short if they read something that doesn't sound right in their home language. For this reason, we have to help students become fluent in the syntax of book language.

Debbie is reminded of an experience from her days as a junior high school English teacher preparing students for a district-wide grammar and usage test. You know the kind: "Which is correct? *I have lain out in the sun all afternoon*, or *I have laid out in the sun all afternoon*. One usually weak student answered every question correctly, even indicating that "I have lain . . ." was correct. Inwardly praising herself for her stellar teaching, Debbie asked the student how he knew all those answers. Her ego was quickly deflated by his answer: "Oh, on these grammar tests I always mark the answers that don't sound right."

Again, formal, standard English does not always sound right to our students. We must help them with the language of books.

Graphophonics

The graphophonic information system refers to the print (*grapho–*) and corresponding sound (*–phonic*) combinations of words. In order to construct meaning and read with fluency, readers must know how words work. Graphophonic information focuses on using all this knowledge flexibly:

- letter-sound relationships in English words from our Anglo-Saxon heritage (e.g., *j* is pronounced /j/ as in *judge.*)

- letter-sound relationships in words borrowed from other languages, (e.g., *j* is pronounced /w/ as in *Juan.*)

- patterns and clusters of letters in English words from our Anglo-Saxon heritage (e.g., *can*)

- patterns and clusters of letters from words borrowed from other languages (e.g., *canal*)

- patterns and clusters of letters that change pronunciation (e.g., *ei* of *eiderdown* and *eight*, the *–ild* of *child* and *children)*

- prefixes, including those with Latin and Greek meanings (e.g., *pre–* as in *presume* or *preview*)

- suffixes, including both inflectional endings and meaning-based endings (e.g., the *–ing* of *swinging* or the *–ment* of *establishment)*

- root words and how their pronunciation changes (e.g., *medic* or *medical* and *medicine*)

- spelling changes (e.g., *policy* to *policies*)

- patterns in English syllables (e.g., ta/ble)

- patterns in syllables derived from other languages (e.g., tab/leau)

A reader must be able to deal with unfamiliar multisyllable words by trying these strategies:

- taking the word apart, looking for familiar patterns or chunks of letters (e.g., un/think/able), putting those parts together, then using meaning and syntax as well as sound to see if this word is in one's oral vocabulary

- If it is not, the reader must remember that he or she has given it an approximate, temporary pronunciation. The reader uses context clues to determine its meaning (e.g., "con/fra/ter/ni/ty = con + fraternity. Con– as a prefix can mean either *against* or *with*. In this passage, the group of people seem to be working together, so a *confraternity* must be a band of people who work together.")

- making analogies to known words and then reading across the target word with accuracy (e.g., "I know *stereophonic* means two speakers, so *monophonic* must mean one speaker.")

Using the visual system alone is not enough. Yes, readers must be able to read the words with a high degree of accuracy and consistency. Those of you who know how to read French or Spanish, however, realize your pronunciation may not be perfectly correct. So it is with avid readers in English whose reading vocabulary far outstrips their spoken vocabulary. (We won't mention embarrassing moments when we've said the right word aloud, only to realize we've put the accent on the wrong syllable. Ask <u>Deb</u>-or-ah sometime about her incorrect public pronunciation of de-<u>ba</u>-cle.) Readers must know what the words mean or derive their meaning from the context of the words in a passage to be readers and not simply word callers.

Punctuation and capitalization are also a part of the graphophonic information system. Knowing what the punctuation signifies—i.e., a stop at a period, a pause at a comma—is key to understanding the nuances of the text's meaning. As students encounter punctuation, they must be shown how it affects the reading of the text. Another aspect of this visual system is graphic presentation or layout. As readers change genres, they must use the graphic presentation of a text to help them understand it. Here are some visual aspects a reader must negotiate:

- The text in a novel is configured in a different way on the page from that in a multicolumn expository text. Readers need to know how to negotiate the columns with their headings and subheadings.

- Pictures in a novel provide no new information to the story; they merely represent scenes from the story. Pictures, graphs, and charts in an expository text do present new information that cannot be found in the extended text. A reader must make connections between the facts presented by the pictures and charts and some aspect of the information presented in the extended text.

- Novels do not have summaries at the end of chapters, while many textbooks do. Readers need to know how to use the summaries to check their understanding of what they have read.

- Novels frequently include dialogue that is punctuated and paragraphed in specific ways to indicate a change in speakers. Figuring out which character is talking can be a challenge for a fledgling reader who has not learned that authors present speech in various ways—sometimes with quotation marks and the name of the character, yet at other times without such clarifying information.

- Poetry is formatted in endless ways. Poems may be shaped according to their subject (concrete poems) or may follow very strict rules about the number of lines and syllables, as in haiku. They may tell an extended story and consist of scenes (e.g., epic poems such as *The Odyssey*) or they may follow the rules of an Elizabethan sonnet. Readers must use cues from the format of the poem to help them understand its meaning.

- The formats used in nonfiction present rich visual information, but the formats differ by subject. Math books are formatted in different ways than social studies books. Scientific studies are written according to a set structure, while an article about natural phenomenon in *National Geographic* will use a different format. Readers must be able to flexibly negotiate these various formats.

In the appendix on pages 168–175, we provide charts with prompts to use for the difficulties readers in grades 3–8 typically encounter. These charts present language you can use during guided practice that will help you to walk that fine line between supporting students when they really need help, yet doing so in a way that leads them to do their own thinking and encourages independence. We never want to become a "crutch" for students.

A Note From Ann

Knowing what to say to students as they struggle with a text, and when to say it, is a teaching skill that takes time to develop—and patience with oneself! I always found it helpful to think about my students and which prompts I would most likely use with a particular group as I planned a lesson. Then I would include an abbreviated version of these prompts in my plan. This helped me to use prompts that were most appropriate for the group and to avoid jumping in too soon as students were thinking through how to solve a problem. I would also take some time after the lesson to reflect back on what happened between my students and me during the lesson. What concepts, language, text structures, and vocabulary challenged the students? How did I intervene? Did I provide too much or too little assistance? After I prompted students, did they seem to begin to take on the strategic thinking of these prompts? What would be the next step instructionally for these students? Time spent planning and reflecting on the teaching and learning will ensure that your lessons are efficient and effective.

Distinguishing Guided Practice From Other Types of Small-Group Instruction

"Guided" as well as "leveled text" have become buzz words in the world of education; they are linked to a wide variety of materials and programs for instruction, especially by publishing executives who are anxious to provide and sell materials that reflect the latest fad in teaching. We want to clarify what guided practice *is* and *is not* for the purposes of this book. Jeff Williams, a literacy coach/consultant in Solon, Ohio, has shared the lists of descriptors in the boxes on the next page.

Guided Practice is

- a teaching/learning opportunity in a classroom

- a small-group instructional opportunity involving no more than 4–6 students

- an outgrowth of a teacher's detailed knowledge of a group of students and their literacy development, with an eye toward placing children in groups that best meet their needs

- a context for using all types of texts—poetry, chapter books, newspaper or magazine articles, non-fiction texts or textbooks

- a time to

  - observe students closely

  - prompt them to make sense of the text

  - teach them strategies for processing text

  - provide students with feedback about their use of strategies as they read

- a means for encouraging students to take on more of the responsibility for doing the work, while the teacher varies his or her own involvement according to the students' needs

- an opportunity for helping students become more proficient and independent in their use of strategies with feedback from the teacher as needed

- interaction between students and the teacher and among students as they read to understand the text, confirm or revise predictions, make connections, ask questions, make inferences, draw conclusions, summarize meaning, and personally respond to the message of the text

Guided Practice is not

- teaching the story or text

- "round-robin" reading

- literature circles

- the same for every group

- groups of more than 6

- inflexible groupings of students

- testing students' knowledge of a book

- always followed up with writing—other means of follow-up can be discussion, rereading, reading related texts, an artistic response, or more writing

- easy to implement

Guided practice is appropriate for readers at any level. The next section contains examples of guided practice at the primary, intermediate, and middle school levels.

Example 1:
Guided Practice in the Primary Classroom

Once students have mastered the early literacy behaviors of directionality, one-to-one matching of voice to printed words, and recognition of a few sight words, they are ready to engage in small-group guided practice.

A first-grade teacher gathers a small group of students at a U-shaped table. He sits in the U so that he can observe and interact with each student throughout the lesson. He has chosen a nonfiction Level E text (leveled per Fountas and Pinnell's system) titled *The Sun* by Brenda Parkes. The teacher has been working with this group on cross-checking the first letter of words against the meaning of the text, which at this level is often contained in the pictures. The students have been able to cross-check successfully with teacher prompts. His focus for today's lesson is to have students self-monitor their reading and self-correct errors by cross-checking the initial letter of a word against the meaning of the text.

After providing an introduction to the meaning framework of the text and the basic sentence structure, the teacher asks students to predict and locate the word *warm* by saying, *What would you expect to see at the beginning of the word* warm? The students repeat the word, listening for the first sound, and identify the first letter as *w.* The teacher praises them for saying the word slowly to themselves so they can hear that first sound and asks them to locate the word and frame it using their two index fingers.

With the support of this helpful introduction, the students read the entire book independently. The teacher leans toward each of the group members in turn and listens to their reading, observing how each student processes the text. Keeping in mind his goal of encouraging students to self-monitor and self-correct, he offers as little support as possible, offering the occasional prompt and increasing his help only when it's evident that a student cannot do the reading independently.

Students know to reread the text if they finish before the other students. Once everyone in the group has read the book at least once, the teacher has students retell what they have read. He asks open-ended questions, such as, *Why is the sun important?* to help students think beyond the text.

The teacher then chooses one or two examples of student work that demonstrates self-monitoring, cross-checking, and self-correcting. He praises the work and the efforts behind it, offering positive reinforcement to the entire group.

Example 2:
Guided Practice in the Intermediate Classroom

Guided practice at the intermediate level provides students with the skills and strategies to deal with the challenges of more complex text.

During recent read-alouds and shared practice with her students, a fourth-grade teacher has focused on how to use the features of nonfiction text to deepen students' understanding of a subject. She has pulled together a group of students who has struggled with reading and getting information from content area text. She has chosen a Level O text, *Platypuses* by Alexandra Boow. The book, an unusual blend of both fiction and nonfiction, uses letters from a fictional zoologist researching the platypus to frame the sections of text. The letters are to his grandchildren, who are working on a science project about the animal. The teacher hopes the book will make learning about the platypus more accessible to readers who struggle with processing the information in nonfiction texts. The letters clearly identify the main idea for each section of the book. The teacher plans a dual focus for guided practice with this group:

1. To assist students in asking questions about a text and searching for the answers to these questions by reading the text and processing the information presented in the headings, charts, and maps

2. To guide students to read unknown words by flexibly using a variety of word-solving strategies

The teacher begins by setting up a K-W-L chart on an easel to record what students already know about platypuses (K), what they expect to learn by reading the book (W), and what they have learned after reading and collecting information from the text (L). Sharing what they know in the K column helps students activate and share any prior knowledge they have about platypuses. To generate questions for the W column, the teacher directs students to work with a partner to look at the table of contents and headings and think about what questions the book may answer. The pairs talk and suggest questions like the following: *Is a platypus a mammal or reptile? Where do platypuses live? What do they eat?* The teacher records these in the W column.

As students follow along, the teacher then reads aloud the first two pages of the text: page 2, the first letter from Grandpa; and page 3, the first section of the text under the heading *Mammal or Reptile?* Page 3 also includes a chart for comparing characteristics of different animals, including the platypus. The group talks about the letter from Grandpa, which clarifies the purpose of these letters in the book. They also discuss the first section of information about the platypus. Since the teacher has demonstrated how to read charts in a nonfiction text, she asks the partner groups to summarize the information in the chart. Students notice that the platypus shares some character-istics with birds, mammals, and reptiles, but they have the most in common with mammals. The teacher asks them which question in the K-W-L chart they have already found the answer for, and they identify the first question, *Is a platypus a mammal or reptile?* The teacher then asks students to dictate the answer to that question, which she records in the L column.

The teacher then assigns students to independently read the next section of the book (pages 4–11) and record in their reading notebooks the answers to other questions on the K-W-L chart. As students read, the teacher listens in to each student individually, asking him or her to read in a voice loud enough for her to hear but not so loud that it disturbs the others in the group. She knows that some words in this section, like *electrical, stomachs, poison,* and *silvery,* will be difficult for this group. She observes how each student self-monitors, cross-checks, searches to solve tricky words, and self-corrects errors. She notes their fluency and only intervenes to prompt students when they cannot solve a word on their own. One student has trouble with the word *silvery,* so she quickly writes the word on a whiteboard, leaving space between the chunks—sil-<u>ver</u>-<u>y</u>—and asks him to first read each part separately and then read quickly across all parts of the word. The teacher then prompts the student to reread the sentence, checking to be sure the word now makes sense and sounds right. The student confirms that it does. As she works with each of the other students, the teacher notices that some are successfully solving words using the many strategies the class has worked on, while others continue to struggle. She makes a note to remind herself of which students need a mini-lesson refresher on solving unfamiliar words.

The lesson has taken about 25 minutes, so the teacher dismisses the students and tells them to finish the reading and writing on their own. Tomorrow she will call the group together again to summarize what they have learned about the platypus and will record their findings in the L-column of the chart.

Example 3:
Guided Practice in a Middle School Classroom

Middle school students still need small-group guided practice that focuses on the new challenges and complexities of more sophisticated fiction and nonfiction text.

The seventh-grade teacher has noticed during the reading workshop time that several students have difficulty making sense of dialogue in the stories and novels they are reading. They can't follow who is talking or picture the emotions expressed by the speakers or understand how the action of the story is being furthered by the dialogue. When asked to read a passage of dialogue aloud, their reading is flat, almost monotone with no break between speakers. Because the class is focusing on a theme of survival, the teacher uses the short story "The Most Dangerous Game" by Richard Connell (1990) from the class's literature book for guided practice. The students have read the story earlier in the year, so the material is familiar. The teacher calls over four students to work with her while the other students are engaged in independent reading.

The teacher draws a line down a piece of chart paper to make an impromptu comparison chart. After jotting "Rainsford" at the top of the first column and "The General" at the top of the second column, she has the students brainstorm all they can remember about the two characters in 45 seconds. She listens and jots descriptors in the chart as she hears them.

The teacher tells students they are going to practice reading so they can hear the distinct voices of the two antagonists in the story. She hands each of them a copy of page 69 of their literature book, where the "most dangerous game" is introduced. She hands two students yellow highlighters and tells them that each is now the character of Rainsford. She hands the other two students orange highlighters and tells them that each is the character of the General. As they read the following short excerpt, their job is to highlight the exact words that their character is saying:

"You have some wonderful heads here," said Rainsford as he ate a particularly well-cooked filet mignon. "That Cape buffalo is the largest I ever saw."

"Oh, that fellow. Yes, he was a monster."

"Did he charge you?"

"Hurled me against a tree," said the general. "Fractured my skull, but I got the brute."

"I've always thought," said Rainsford, "that the Cape buffalo is the most dangerous of all big game."

The teacher gives students a few minutes to read through the dialogue individually, and then she has the two Rainsfords sit together and the two Generals sit together to work out which words to highlight. She listens to their discussions and prompts with the following questions: *How do you know? What clues did the author give you? How do you picture this scene? What tone of voice would your character use?*

When the pairs are confident in their color-coding, the teacher asks what they notice about the punctuation and paragraphing that helped them distinguish speakers. The students identify these clues with a little help from the teacher:

- quotation marks right before and right after the exact words

- identification of the speaker through the phrases "said Rainsford" and "said the general"

- new paragraphs when the speaker changes

The teacher then matches a Rainsford with a General and has them read their lines as though they were reading a play, focusing on the tone of voice the characters would probably use. She listens in as they practice, noting aloud what she is visualizing about the scene based on their reading. Each pair wants to read their "play" for the other, so they do. One of the Generals lounges in his chair and pantomimes smoking a cigar and sipping wine while he talks. This student is obviously visualizing the after-dinner conversation.

The teacher sends the Rainsfords and the Generals back to their seats with their highlighters and asks them to mark their parts in the remaining dialogue on the page. She sets an appointment with them for the next day to come and read their parts on that page as a follow-up. She posts the list of authors' clues for speaker changes so that they can refer to it as they work. The teacher knows she'll need to plan additional guided practice for them using other selections, but she knows that short, successful practices are more beneficial than single, intense sessions.

What is the Tipping Point in Guided Practice?

In *The Tipping Point,* Malcolm Gladwell explores the "stickiness" of a message, or what makes a message memorable. In our context, we have to ask ourselves what makes our teaching point memorable? How can we be sure our students will remember our lesson after the test, or even after they've left our guided practice session? Gladwell says that a message must be *practical* and *personal* in order to be "sticky" (page 98). In guided practice, we can make our lesson both practical and personal to the individuals within these small groups. How will what we are teaching help students *in a practical way* with what they want to do right now? How can we make it *personal* through our choice of materials and examples?

One of our colleagues poses math problems that have the feel of brainteasers, yet they are written using students' names, the names of their siblings, and the names of their favorite teachers. The scenarios posed in the math problems are ones facing students as they shop at the mall or decide what to buy for lunch. Students readily picture what is happening in these story problems because they or their friends are the main characters. The situations are familiar and personal. The math lesson becomes memorable.

In Chapter 1, we discussed Gladwell's account of the research that went into ensuring the success of *Blues Clues*. The conclusions drawn from this research apply well to guided practice. The reading work that students do must be complex enough to engage their interest yet easy enough to ensure success. To be effective, teachers must strike a balance between what students know and what is new and challenging throughout the lesson. This balancing act comes into play before the lesson as the teacher chooses materials, during the lesson as the teacher guides and prompts, and after the lesson as the teacher decides what teaching point will best help this group continue to progress as readers.

In guided practice, we teachers choose the materials to use in our lessons. Content-area texts are often too difficult for most students to read, even with teacher guidance. Many publishing companies, including Newbridge and National Geographic, provide supplemental texts that present content-area information written on a variety of reading levels. These texts can be used with groups in guided practice. We can choose materials that are topical (articles from the newspaper, a Web site, a teen magazine). Through our choice of materials, we can tailor our lessons to our students' interests, while making certain that the materials are at an appropriate reading level. We can pose an engaging problem using familiar or easy materials.

As we plan our guided practice, we can adjust the sequence and duration of lessons to the unique needs of our students. Gladwell says, "Those who are successful at creating social epidemics do not just do what they think is right. They deliberately test their interventions." (Gladwell, page 258) In guided practice, we do not blindly follow page after page of lessons written by some distant author. We have a teaching point in mind, we make our lessons practical and personal, and we assess whether they are successful. If the proverbial lightbulb turns on, we move to the next thing students need. If it remains dark, we find another way to address our teaching point. The literacy epidemic can spread quickly if we are responsive to our students.

Planning for Teaching That is Responsive

Because it is essential that our instruction during guided practice is responsive to our students, we cannot plan every step in the teaching/learning process. Guided practice cannot follow a prescribed script. However, some planning and reflection is required to ensure that the guidance we offer during the lesson provides students with what they *currently* need in order to continue to progress as readers. Effective, efficient planning and implementation include these five basic steps:

1. **Framing the lesson**: What is my purpose for this lesson with this group of students? What is my task in carrying out this purpose? How will I play my roles as maven, salesperson, and connector?

2. **Determining one or two teaching points**: What message do I want my students to take away from this lesson? What do I want my students to be able to do—not just with this text but with other texts the student will read—as a result of the guidance I will be providing during this lesson?

3. Choosing appropriate and key activities and prompts: Which student behaviors will I focus on while reading this text? What prompts will I use to engage students in the strategic thinking they will do to effectively read this text? What will I bring from my own experiences and knowledge of students to make the message "sticky"? How will I make it personal and practical? How will I use repetition? In what ways will students actively respond?

A Note From Ann

Educators across the country are struggling to meet the requirements of the legislation of No Child Left Behind (NCLB) and the Individuals with Disabilities Education Improvement Act (IDEA) of 2004. The use of research-based instruction and data-driven interventions are basic features of the requirements in this legislation. Response to Intervention (RTI) is a model proposed by IDEA 2004 for identifying struggling learners and determining their instructional needs. RTI is a general education initiative that places the responsibility for providing effective instruction for struggling students squarely on the shoulders of classroom teachers. Richard Allington and Sean Walmsley in the preface of the RTI edition (2007) of *No Quick Fix* describe the challenge for teachers in fulfilling this responsibility:

> . . . the key to an effective RTI plan is to provide the targeted, specific instruction that each student needs. No two students ever have identical instruction needs. The success of any RTI initiative will rest largely on the ability of the teachers to select appropriate instructional activities based on the diagnostic evidence each student provides at the onset and throughout the intervention.

How can teachers meet the diverse needs of the students in their classrooms knowing that each learner is unique in what he or she brings to the teaching/learning situation and in how he or she takes on new learning? Guided practice provides a viable answer to this question. It is assessment-based instruction that works on the cutting edge of students' learning and is responsive to their unique needs as they work with their teacher in small, flexible groups.

Grouping is an efficient means of meeting the needs of students in a classroom. However, for the instruction to be on the cutting edge of our students' learning, we must group students by thoughtfully considering our assessments of their instructional needs and flexibly adjusting to changes in each student's learning over time. One of the wonderful benefits of guided practice is that it allows teachers to focus on individual students within a group. Once students have been introduced to a new book chosen by the teacher, they read that book, or sections of it, to themselves. The teacher can then listen in on the reading of two or three students and respond appropriately to individual students, making on-the-spot decisions about what feedback each needs in order to continue to learn and develop as readers. This can also be a time when the teacher conducts a brief assessment of a student's oral reading and retelling of a small section of the text. These individual interactions provide the teacher with specific information about how this group of students is taking on and practicing new learning. Since students with similar instructional needs are grouped together, they often have similar difficulties with processing text. The teacher can guide each student individually while the group is reading a portion of the text and then make a decision as to which strategy or skill to set as a priority for all the students in the group. After the reading and discussion of the text, the teacher can focus on one or two teaching points to address the difficulties the group has had.

4. **Assessing student learning**: How will I know that students have successfully taken on new learning? What invitations or suggestions could I give students to extend their learning?

5. **Reflecting after the lesson**: How did the lesson go? What happened? What didn't happen that should have? How will I tweak the message or its delivery to make it "stickier"? What should happen next? How have students progressed over time? Am I recognizing and celebrating their efforts, even when the results aren't perfect? Have I kept the long-term goals for these students in mind or am I getting caught up in the details?

Planning should never be in such detail that your responsiveness to students is preempted by the plan. Indeed, a key characteristic of guided practice is that the teacher's keen observation of students facilitates the give and take between students and teacher that reflects the particular ways in which *these* students interact with and respond to *this* text. It's this unique responsiveness that defines the quality and effect of the teaching and learning that happens during guided practice. See the appendix (pages 165–166) for questions to assist you as you plan for a specific group of students.

Teachers at the same grade level in upper elementary level or in the same or related content areas at the middle school level can plan with each other. Mapping out the content and processes and matching up the texts can be a huge job. Working together, teachers can accomplish this more efficiently and more effectively.

Solutions to the Dilemma of Finding Materials Appropriate for Guided Practice

It can be a challenge to find quality leveled text for guided practice, especially if you are looking for nonfiction text to use for content-area instruction. Fortunately, many publishing companies have responded to this need and have supplied well-written texts dealing with content-area topics at various reading levels. Below are Web sites for companies Ann has used.

Scholastic: www.scholastic.com

National Geographic: www.ngsp.com

Heinemann: www.heinemann.com

Newbridge: www.newbridgeonline.com

Reading A–Z: www.readinga-z.com

Many school districts are making the shift from using textbooks exclusively to providing teachers with multiple copies of multilevel texts across content-area subjects. With these supplemental texts, teachers can engage students in learning content and process simultaneously. Using nonfiction texts for guided practice helps to build the background knowledge students need in order to read content-area textbooks that are often written above their grade level.

Making Do When Leveled Text is Not Available

School districts often adopt a textbook or program that is chosen by a majority of teachers or the dictates of the administration. What can a teacher do if the only materials available are a published, basal-type program with script for instruction? How can a teacher make thoughtful use of such a program, allowing students to do the thinking and being responsive to them during guided practice? The following is a list of some ways to make the best use of a published program:

- Use the teacher's guide provided as a resource as you plan and prepare for your students. Think about what your students know and what they need to know as you pick and choose among the activities suggested. Think of the teacher's edition as a kind of menu. You wouldn't order everything off a menu for a single meal. It wouldn't be healthy, you wouldn't have the money, and you certainly wouldn't have the stomach or the time to eat it all.

- If you are teaching a strategy, prepare for instruction by reading the text beforehand and thinking about how *you* use this strategy as you read and how *you* think and process the text to understand the author's message. Note which strategies suggested by the authors help you and which seem cumbersome or inappropriate. What are the differences between your approach and the author's approach? How can you help your students understand that what works for one reader may not work for another? How can you teach for flexibility?

- Plan for opportunities to allow students to share their thinking so you can be responsive to their processing of text.

- If the basal provides only an excerpt of a book, find the book and read it in its entirety with students. You can read aloud some of the text or use shared reading for parts of the text by putting it on an overhead projector if there are not enough copies available. If you can't use the whole book for modeling or for shared or guided practice, consider using the excerpt from the basal as an invitation for independent reading or for book clubs.

Echoes Across Curricular Areas

Students need instruction and practice in reading texts of all kinds. Once they have learned how to think strategically and to use problem-solving strategies in different subject areas through teacher read-alouds and shared practice, students need opportunities to practice and apply these strategies themselves, yet still have the teacher's guidance when necessary.

Guided practice provides the means to support students' reading of all types of texts: novels, newspaper articles, journals, poetry, biographies, science or social studies texts, and word problems in math. Although the content and structure of texts across subject areas differ, the interactions between teacher and students as they read these texts bear many similarities. The clear message to students here is, "You do, I help." And all students are reading, whether they are reading to themselves, to a peer, or to the teacher. It is *not* round-robin reading with one student reading and the other students listening!

In Chapter 3, we showed a chart comparing what teachers say across subject areas to engage students in thinking and problem solving (page 78). Using the example from this chart of visualizing and predicting, here's what a reading, math, and music teacher might say before, during, and after a learning activity to shift the responsibility onto students for doing the thinking and problem solving and to guide them in the process:

	WHAT A READING TEACHER MIGHT SAY:	WHAT A MATH TEACHER MIGHT SAY:	WHAT A MUSIC TEACHER MIGHT SAY:
BEFORE	As you read, use your imagination to visualize what's happening in the story. Use your senses to see, hear, taste, smell, and feel and with these clues predict what will happen next.	As you read the story problem, visualize the details of the problem in your head. Put yourself into the problem so you can see what it involves in your mind's eye and estimate the answer based on this thinking.	Listen in your mind as you scan the music. Use clues to predict how the melody and the accompaniment probably sound.
DURING	• What senses are you using as you read this text? • Reread this section and visualize what is happening and make predictions about what will happen next. • Write your predictions on sticky notes and place them in the part of the text where you are making them.	• Work the problem out to see if the answer you get is close to the estimate you made.	• Play through the music to see if it matches what you heard in your mind.
AFTER	• Look back at the predictions you made throughout the text. • Were your predictions confirmed or not? • If they were not, reread to see what misled you. • Make new predictions about what will happen next.	• If the answer is not close to your estimate, go back and think about the problem details and rework the answer. • Check your answer to see if it makes sense.	• If there is a mismatch between what you heard in your mind and what it sounded like as you played the music, go back to the problem area and figure out what clues misled you. • Replay the music to confirm your thinking.

Problem-solving similarities among reading, math, and music

Throughout the planning and implementation of a guided practice lesson, we support students' thinking and problem solving. Students do the reading work, but we help them through our choice of materials, specific tasks, and our supportive prompts. Our goal is to develop independent, self-extending readers who can construct meaning from the variety of texts they encounter in and out of school.

Change Over Time and Across Developmental Levels

During the guided practice stage of the gradual release model, students are transitioning from being dependent on the teacher to becoming independent, self-extending readers. Our goal is to facilitate this developing independence. We accomplish this by doing the following:

- determining the teaching point for a group that will reinforce their learning and shift their level of proficiency

- choosing text that is at an appropriate level for our students while also providing opportunities for teaching and learning

- considering which prompts to use for a particular group of students at this point in their learning

- preparing an introduction to the text that will support students' successful processing of that text without preempting occasions for them to solve problems and extend learning on their own

- thinking ahead about what's next for these students

For students at the primary level, who are just learning how print works and what readers do as they read, there are multiple dimensions of teaching and learning. Some examples of these are one-to-one correspondence related to the concept of a word, directionality, locating known words, self-monitoring, self-correction, and fluency. The teacher, as the "knowledgeable other" and guide, makes many decisions across guided practice lessons in order to help students develop increasing control over all dimensions of literacy learning. He or she begins by carefully selecting books that have enough familiar vocabulary and language structure as well as picture support to allow students to read much of the text with ease. The teacher also considers what students are learning about reading now and looks for text that fosters that learning. If the text is too easy, students won't learn anything new. If there are too many challenges, they will be overwhelmed and frustrated. In *Becoming Literate* (1991), Marie Clay addresses the importance of this balance between familiar and new, stating that learning occurs when a student uses texts "which allow him to practice and develop the full range of strategies which he does control, and by problem-solving new challenges, reach out beyond that present control" (Clay, 1993a, p. 215). Finding text that provides this balance is the basis for accelerating students' learning.

Let's say, for example, that a first-grade teacher wants her emerging readers to learn to self-monitor. She has been teaching these students how to cross-check the first letter of a word in a sentence against the picture in order to solve the word. She will choose a text that includes vocabulary and language structure that is mostly familiar to students, but she also wants to be sure there are words students haven't seen before but that they can solve by using this cross-checking strategy. The teacher introduces the book by presenting its overall message and attending to any unusual language structure in the text. She will also choose one or two words for the students to find, asking them, "What would you expect to see at the beginning of __ (saying the chosen word)?" This reinforces the strategy of checking the first letter of the word against the sound at the beginning of the word and sets students up to apply this strategy as they read. Then as students read the text, the teacher watches to see how they deal with new words they encounter and whether or not they apply what they have learned about cross-checking. When students need some help, the teacher will prompt accordingly and, based on her observations, plan for a teaching point after they read that will support all students in the group.

At the intermediate and middle school levels, there is a dual focus for teachers: helping students to learn how to read text and learn content. More often than not, textbooks for grades 3–8 are written above grade level and are difficult for most students to read on their own. To compound this dilemma, state departments present teachers with sets of standards that must be met. Intermediate-level teachers often have to teach many content areas, each with its particular set of standards. Middle school teachers are usually departmentalized, but they are faced with a vast set of standards required in their content area. There just never seems to be enough time in the day to accomplish all that! What can teachers do to efficiently and effectively teach their students how to read content-area text as well as to learn content?

The choice of text and the introduction to the text are means to "level the playing field" for intermediate and middle school students who struggle to read content-area text. Here are some ways in which teachers of grades 3–8 can support both students' reading development and learning of content:

- Build background knowledge before reading difficult text through read-alouds and shared practice with content-related text

- Create a K-W-L chart listing what students already know about a subject, what they want to learn, and leaving space to list what they have learned after reading

- Use supplemental text that deals with grade-level content but that is written at a level students can read with guidance (see page 104 for Web sites for book companies that publish these texts)

- Introduce students to the features of content-area text using leveled supplemental text and demonstrate how these features can be used to support comprehension

- Preview a text with students, encouraging them to look at the title, subtitle, headings, subheadings, pictures and captions, graphs, charts, and maps and then list questions about these features

- List questions to be answered as students read

- Provide a double-entry journal for students to use while they read and demonstrate how to use it with the text, writing a notable quote on one side and what you think about it on the other side

Choosing text carefully and setting up a lesson to provide students with opportunities to apply new learning enables you to push the boundaries of your students' learning and establish their confidence and independence as a readers.

Possible Solutions to Management and Behavioral Issues

The first question teachers ask when learning about guided practice is, "How do I manage students who are not in my guided reading group?" It's a good question. With the limited time in the classroom day, we certainly want students to be engaged in constructive learning activities as much as possible. During literacy block, students should participate in whole-group, small-group, and independent learning. When a teacher's attention is focused on a guided-practice group, the other students should be working independently or with a partner, practicing and applying new learning.

A classroom structure that engages students in independent work and frees the teacher to focus on small-group guided practice is what Debbie Diller calls work stations. Work stations are areas in the classroom in which students can work alone or with a partner to practice and apply what the teacher has modeled or taught during read-alouds, shared practice, and guided practice. The materials in the work station have been used first for instruction, so students are familiar with them. Also, the materials are differentiated so that students at different reading levels and with different needs can do similar activities at a station yet function at their own learning level. In essence, the work stations provide purposeful and appropriate practice for all students.

These work stations can be flexibly used to develop literacy skills and strategies across content areas. In her book *Practice With Purpose, Literacy Work Stations for Grades 3–6* (2005), Diller presents a wide variety of work stations appropriate for intermediate and middle school students. Some relate to reading and writing, while others relate to science or social studies, such as note taking, creating quiz cards about a topic, using specific content vocabulary, doing a quick-write, and investigating a culture. Diller emphasizes the importance of designing work stations that follow up on instruction, introducing stations one at a time, modeling and having students model how the station works, making "I Can" lists of activities appropriate for a station, and continually debriefing together to solve problems and keep the stations running smoothly.

When students are not working with the teacher in a guided practice group, this is an opportune time to read independently and respond to text. Many teachers have students keep a literacy notebook to record the titles of the books they are reading, the genre, and their thoughts and reactions to what they have read. This provides teachers with a way to oversee how much independent reading the students are doing, the kind of texts they are choosing, and their thinking as they are reading. The teacher can use this notebook during individual conferences with students to support and broaden their independent reading. In Chapter 5, we further explore independent reading and its importance in the apprenticeship model.

Through mini-lessons, teachers can establish the culture of the classroom and prepare students to work independently so they can focus on a guided reading group. In *Guiding Readers and Writers, Grades 3–6*, Fountas and Pinnell present a series of mini-lessons for the first 20 days of a school year that help students understand their role and responsibilities during the literacy block. These mini-lessons address management issues, such as choosing just right books and buzzing about their reading; literacy strategies and skills, such as self-monitoring and solving unknown words; and literary analysis, such as distinguishing the genre of a text. These mini-lessons are the oil that keeps the classroom machinery working smoothly, and they need to continue throughout the school year as issues and problems arise.

With teacher modeling, students will understand and take on their roles and responsibilities. It's also effective to have students model for each other.

Nothing is more disruptive than having students interrupt a guided reading group when they don't understand something. One teacher emphasized to her students that she was the last resort when they were stuck. "Ask three before you ask me!" was her mantra. Giving students a set of options to try before interrupting the teacher works well. Here are a few:

- See if you can get along despite the problem—i.e., skip the word, try another book.

- Try to help yourself first by self-monitoring. Ask yourself: *What would make sense? Do I know something that would help me?*

- Go to one or two peers who probably know (as long as they are not in the guided reading group)

- Final resort—ask the teacher.

Being sure that all books and materials are readily available and that students know what their tasks are is the best way to avoid these interruptions.

As part of the learning community, students should be involved in evaluating their own behavior and in brainstorming ways to keep things running smoothly. Jeff Williams, literary coach and consultant for Solon City Schools in Solon, Ohio, devised a rubric for students to use at the end of the literacy block as a measure of how things went. Once the rubric is completed, the class discusses how well it did, describing why things did or did not go well and how everyone could help to improve. This makes clear to students that it's their job to create a culture conducive to learning as well as to solve problems that arise. Students often come up with creative solutions to problems and take on the responsibility to make it happen.

To Sum it Up

In guided practice, the teacher hands over to students the responsibility for reading and thinking. Students are actively engaged in reading text at a level that presents just enough opportunity for problem solving, allowing them to apply and practice new learning and to extend their skill as readers. In this phase, the teacher takes on the role of observer and guide. Often, he or she just watches, giving students time to think strategically and to independently solve problems encountered in text. At other times, the teacher decides that students need assistance yet calibrates the level of support he or she gives students according to what he or she knows students can do, or can almost do, themselves. This guidance helps direct the students' thinking toward effective processing of the concepts, language, and vocabulary in the text.

In Chapter 4, we applied the concepts of Malcolm Gladwell's *The Tipping Point* to guided practice as well.

- We explored how the choice of text was a way to make learning both personal and practical. When we choose books that pique and broaden students' interests and that relate to their lives, we make our lessons personal. To ensure that students are successful, we use text with a balance between familiar concepts, language, and vocabulary that students control, and those that provide opportunities for students to successfully solve problems and extend their learning.

- We saw how the teaching and prompting we do in guided practice is practical because it supports thinking and problem solving with what students are currently reading as well as with texts they will read later on.

- We make our guidance personal by observing individuals in a group and tailoring our level of support to our knowledge of each student's level of development.

- We reflect back on lessons to plan thoughtfully for the next lesson and to ensure we are being responsive to changes in our students' development over time.

CHAPTER 4 FOLLOW-UP

A Close-up Look at a Sample Guided Practice Lesson

We can meet the needs and build on the strengths of every student in our classroom by planning and preparing for guided practice. This means:

- knowing our students as readers

- grouping them according to instructional need and reading level

- choosing appropriate materials to teach what students are ready to learn

- responding to students before, during, and after reading a text to push the edge of their learning so that what you are guiding them to do today, they will be able to do on their own tomorrow

The focus for guided practice changes from the whole-group instruction of the read-aloud and shared practice in which the teacher is *doing* and the students are *watching* or *helping* to small-group instruction in which the students are *doing* and the teachers is *observing* and *guiding*. In guided practice, the teacher steps to the side and allows students to take on the central role in reading. The teacher is there to observe and to provide guidance when necessary.

Learning for students is both personal and practical because we:

- know our students well and set instructional goals that will push their cutting edge of learning

- choose materials that will provide a balance between giving students the opportunity to practice what they have learned and to deal with new challenges

- encourage students to be independent yet provide appropriate support by prompting them to solve problems as they arise

- respond to individual students during guided practice to provide each one with feedback that builds on his or her individual strengths and meets his or her unique needs.

What follows is a guided practice lesson Ann observed in Sarah Robey's fourth-grade classroom. In this lesson, Sarah uses *Dear Mr. Henshaw* by Beverly Cleary with one of her guided practice groups. The book makes learning personal for her students because the main character is a fourth grader who is coping with a problem that is unfortunately all too common—divorced parents. As you read through Sarah's lesson, look for ways in which she differentiates her teaching and responses to make the lesson personal and practical for the students.

Sample Lesson for a Small Group at the Intermediate Level

This is a group of five capable readers who usually read above grade-level text. However, for this lesson their teacher has chosen *Dear Mr. Henshaw* because it is at a slightly easier level—a beginning fourth-grade-level text. Sarah knows that when students are learning a difficult thinking strategy, it helps to begin with an easier text with familiar concepts, language, and vocabulary. She wants students to be able to think beyond the literal level and discern what the author is implying through the characters and events.

Sarah has introduced the whole class to inferring by thinking aloud during read-alouds and by reading sections of texts together with them during shared practice, prompting students to make their own inferences. A simple T-chart on a large piece of chart paper posted on the board shows their responses.

MY INFERENCE	EVIDENCE FROM TEXT

Inference T-chart

Listed on the chart are the conclusions Sarah and, in some cases, her students have recorded in the first column, and the second column contains a brief statement or two from the text that provides evidence supporting each inference.

Mentor Text: *Dear Mr. Henshaw*

Key teaching point in reading: Readers make inferences while reading by picking up on clues provided by the author and combining those with their background knowledge in order to draw conclusions not explicitly stated in the text.

Content connections:

- *Character development:* Authors create their characters and develop readers' perceptions of these characters through the dialogue, action and description in the text. The measure of a book's appeal to readers often depends on how effectively the author portrays the main characters and how closely the reader relates to them.

- *Letter/diary entry form:* Reading a novel composed of a series of letters and/or diary entries requires readers to adjust their thinking to the characteristics of these forms. The first-person perspective is usually used in letter/diary form, which requires the reader to consider the bias of this perspective.

Lesson Plan Outline

Management: Sarah spent the first 20 days of the school year setting up routines for literacy block, modeling what students should be doing while she is working with a small group in guided practice. Anchor charts titled "How to Choose <u>Just Right</u> Books" or "Can Do" lists at work stations adorn the classroom walls, providing students with easy references to solve problems that might crop up when Sarah is working with a small group. She directs students to begin their independent work in work stations or to spend time reading independently and responding in their reader's notebooks. She then calls the group of five students to the small-group instructional table for guided practice. A fresh copy of the inference T-chart is posted on the board beside the table.

Setting a Purpose: Sarah reminds students of what they have learned about making inferences as they read by saying, "When we make an inference, we are picking up on clues from the story and combining those with our background knowledge to figure out what the author means, without actually stating it." She goes on to explain that authors count on their readers to get to know their characters by making inferences based on what they say or think, what they do, how they are described, and how they relate to other characters in the story.

✔ BEFORE READING

Sarah encourages the group to spend a little time examining the cover of the book and then making some inferences about what it will be about.

Sarah: *Look at the cover of our book and think about the title. Let's start making some inferences about this character whose picture is on the front cover. I'll give you a minute to think and to share with your partner.*

Students study the cover and talk with a partner.

Sarah: *What are some inferences that you have made? Chris?*

Chris: *Rachel and I think the boy is writing something. We think he's writing something about the big truck.*

Sarah: *What's your evidence?*

Chris: *The picture shows a boy writing, and right behind him in the corner is a big truck.*

Sarah: *Great. We'll keep thinking about what inferences we can make all the way through this text. As we read, we will find out more about this boy and about the truck. This will help us to modify our thinking and make even better inferences as we read. All right, we're going to move on. Please read pages 1 and 2 and think about how these pages are written. Be sure to think beyond the words and make some inferences about what is going on.*

Students read page 1 and 2 silently.

Sarah: *What are you noticing about the way page 1 and page 2 are written? What's different about the way they are written than maybe another chapter book that you might pick up?*

Caleb: *It's written in the form of a letter.*

Sarah: *It is written in the form of a letter. We've been talking about how to write a friendly letter this year. Look at page 1. The text has the date, a greeting, the body of a letter, a closing, and a signature. So we're noticing that this is being written in the form of a letter. Who is writing the letters? Rachel?*

Rachel: *The boy whose name is Leigh Botts.*

Sarah: *Leigh Botts is the one writing the letters. So can we say that Leigh is going to be the main character?*

Rachel: *Yes.*

Sarah: *Okay. This book is written a little differently, in the form of letters, and later you're going to see that Leigh also writes in a diary. This book is set up as a series of letters and diary entries. And it's all told from Leigh's point of view. Throughout the book, he is going to go through a lot of changes and challenges in his life. And we're going to learn a lot about him through these letters and diary entries. Who is he writing to?*

Justin: *Mr. Henshaw who is an author.*

Sarah: *Justin, you made an inference there. What evidence did you find to determine that Mr. Henshaw is an author?*

Justin: *In the first letter on page 1, Leigh wrote that his teacher had read Mr. Henshaw's book.*

Sarah writes this inference and evidence on the blank T-chart.

Sarah: *Okay. Mr. Henshaw is an author, and so Leigh Botts is writing letters to this author. Why?*

Susan: *He read a book by Mr. Henshaw so he wanted to write to him, like he was a pen pal.*

Sarah: *That is also an inference. What evidence is there that Leigh is writing to Mr. Henshaw like he is a pen pal?*

Chris: *The title of the book is* <u>Dear Mr. Henshaw</u>, *and all the letters are addressed to him.*

Sarah: *Okay. I think we are ready to read! Please read pages 3–15 and use your individual T-charts to record the inferences you make and the evidence from the book supporting those inferences.*

✔ DURING READING

Students independently read the assigned pages and work on their own T-chart, writing inferences and the evidence from the text to support them. Sarah checks in with Justin and Rachel during this lesson.

Sarah: *Justin, read me page 3, the letter Leigh wrote on November 13, and then we'll talk about some inferences you could make.*

Justin reads page 3 without any errors, but he is unable to make any inferences about the main character or about the letter on the page.

Sarah: *What inferences can you make about Leigh after reading this letter?*

Justin: *Leigh is in fourth grade and is still writing to Mr. Henshaw. Mr. Henshaw did write back to Leigh.*

Sarah: *That's a solid inference. What evidence do you have?*

Justin: *Leigh said he got Mr. Henshaw's answer to his letter, but it was only printed.*

Sarah: *Why did Leigh want Mr. Henshaw to write to him in his own handwriting?*

Justin: *I don't know.*

Sarah: *Reread to yourself the letter before this letter—the one on December 3, and think about what he writes to Mr. Henshaw and why he might want a handwritten letter and not a printed one.*

Justin rereads the previous letter.

Justin: *I don't think he trusts that Mr. Henshaw is really reading his letters and writing back to him. Maybe he thinks Mr. Henshaw is just getting someone like his secretary to send him a letter that's already printed up.*

Guided practice group reading Dear Mr. Henshaw

Sarah: *Good thinking, Justin. Write that on your T-chart and keep reading.*

Sarah has given Justin some individual support. He had some trouble picking out the parts of the letter on page 3 that would provide evidence of Leigh's feelings and his purpose in writing to Mr. Henshaw. Sarah prompted Justin to reread the text in order to understand why the main character was making certain statements in his letters. Rereading is an effective strategy for revisiting text and digging out the meaning.

Now Sarah turns to Rachel, who has read through page 12 and has written three inferences with evidence on her chart. Her third inference is, "Leigh's parents are divorced or at least they live separately." The evidence she cites is, "On page 12, it says that Leigh's mom *'used to say the same thing to Dad when he left his socks on the floor'* and in the P.S. Leigh wrote, *'If my Dad was here, he would tell you to go climb a tree.'* So his dad is not living with him and his mom."

> **Sarah:** *Rachel, you've made an inference and you've used two parts of the text as evidence to support your inference. Authors want their readers to get to know the characters in a story. A reader can often infer how a character is feeling by what he says or does. How do you think Leigh is feeling, based on the last three or four letters he has written to Mr. Henshaw?*

Rachel: *He seems to feel sad and sometimes lonely.*

Sarah: *Okay. Write that as an inference and then reread the last three or four letters to find evidence to support your inference about Leigh's feelings.*

Rachel shows good understanding of what inferences are and is able to provide multiple supporting details and examples of evidence from the text. Sarah prompts Rachel to stretch her thinking so that she can gain a deeper understanding of character development in the story.

The other students in the group have been reading and completing their T-charts. Sarah quickly reviews the other students' charts as the group finishes the reading and writing. She notices that all of the students are able to make inferences and cite at least one piece of evidence. However, none of the students, except Rachel, who had some help, seems to be able to step back from the text and draw conclusions about what kind of a person Leigh is and how he is feeling. Sarah decides to make this the focus of her teaching after the reading.

✔ AFTER READING

Sarah poses open-ended questions about the section of text that students have just read: *What have we learned about Leigh so far? What kind of a person is Mr. Henshaw? What questions do you have about Leigh?* The students discuss these questions. They share their inferences about Leigh and Mr. Henshaw and locate the page and sentence or sentences that support these inferences. Students have noticed that Leigh likes Mr. Henshaw but often gets irritated with him. They've determined that Leigh is living only with his mother and that he moves a lot. However, except for Rachel, the students have not drawn substantive conclusions about what Leigh is like as a character and how he feels about his situation at home and at school.

Echoes: Debriefing Process and Content

Sarah asks the group members to state what they have learned about inferences.

Justin: *Inferences are parts of the story that we make up. We use what the author tells us to make up these parts.*

Chris: *We pick up on clues the author gives us and put these together with what we already know. Then we figure out what the author wants us to know but doesn't actually tell us.*

Sarah: *Putting clues in a novel together with our background knowledge allows us to infer what the author really means.*

Susan: *It makes reading more interesting because you have to keep figuring out what the author means.*

Sarah: *Good point, Susan.*

Sarah explains how authors provide clues to lead readers to get to know the characters in a book.

Sarah: *Boys and girls, you are learning how to make inferences and to support these with statements from the text. This is important in order to get an author's message. Authors want their readers to really get to know their characters. You have read some books this year with characters who seem like your friends by the time you finish reading, correct?*

Chris: *Yeah, I felt like Billy in* <u>Where the Red Fern Grows</u> *was just like my best friend!*

Sarah: *Yes, and the better we know the main people in a story, the better we understand that story and the more we enjoy it! Just like when you meet someone new, it takes time to get to know that person. You learn about the person from what he or she says and does and from what other people say about that person. That's how authors help you to find out about their characters—by what they say and do and by what other characters say about them.*

Susan: *That's why I liked Charlotte in* <u>Charlotte's Web</u> *so much, even though I hate spiders!*

Sarah: *Okay. In this book,* <u>Dear Mr. Henshaw</u>, *Leigh is the main character. We are going to get to know him well as we continue to read. He will also change and grow as a person as the story goes on—just like all children do. As you read, you will be making important inferences about Leigh and how he is feeling. Rachel has an example of such an inference.*

Sarah asks Rachel to share her inference about how Leigh seems to feel sad and lonely by what he writes in his letters. She shares the excerpts from the text that support her conclusion.

Rachel: *We want to get to know characters in a story. We can figure out what they are like and how they are feeling by what they say or do.*

Sarah records these observations on a large piece of construction paper, titled "Making Inferences." She then has her students read the next section of the book and continue adding to their T-charts, encouraging them to refer to the list she has just created.

Your Turn

Regarding the tipping point:

• How did Sarah make this lesson both practical and personal for students?

• How did Sarah ensure that she responded to individual students, giving each the unique feedback that would help him or her grow as a reader?

Regarding the apprenticeship model:

• How did Sarah hand over more responsibility to students for the "doing" during this lesson?

• How did Sarah guide students individually, adjusting the level of support to their individual needs?

Reflecting on the Lesson and Planning for the Next

Sarah jots some quick notes summarizing her observations of the lesson and noting what the next step with this group should be:

- The students are beginning to understand the thinking they do to make inferences while reading.

- They are able to justify their responses in the text.

- These students have learned how authors develop characters in a story and how readers search for clues to better understand its characters and events.

- Plan to meet with the group later in the week when the students will share further entries on their charts.

- Justin may need a little extra guidance in making substantive inferences and finding evidence for them.

- Rachel should be able to apply what she has learned to her independent reading.

Trying it Out: An Invitation

One of the best ways to learn how to teach students in guided practice is to start by working with one student. The dynamics of the teaching and learning will be the same, but the complexity of dealing with multiple groups and multiple students within those groups won't be an issue. It's easier to learn the art and science of guided practice by focusing on one student at a time.

- Begin by doing an assessment with that one student, determining his or her reading level based on word accuracy, fluency, and comprehension. (Pearson's *Developmental Reading Assessments* or Fountas and Pinnell's *Benchmark Assessments* are both excellent tools to use for this purpose.)

- Make a list of how the student can read at that level and what difficulties he or she encountered. Determine three to five areas to focus on to increase the student's use of skills and strategies as a reader. Choose areas that are a priority now for that student.

- Select a short text or portion of a text at the student's reading level that will provide opportunities to practice what he or she has control of, yet will also provide challenges for the student to learn to meet with your support.

- Review the prompts in the chart in the appendix (pages 165–166) and select those that you think will work best for the student.

- Introduce the text and guide as the student reads it, allowing the student to do as much as he or she can independently, prompting the student to problem solve when he or she gets stuck. Make a note or check off the prompts you are using.

- When the student finishes reading, ask him or her to retell what he or she has read and spend some time discussing the text.

- Focus on one or two teaching points that you think are the most important aspects this student needs to learn.

After the lesson, reflect and evaluate by asking yourself the following questions:

- Was your choice of text appropriate for this student? Was he or she able to successfully read most of the text independently? Were there opportunities for the student to do some problem solving?

- Was your prompting helpful to the student? Was the level of prompting helpful in encouraging the student to do the thinking?

- Did the student learn something new? Were your teaching points on his or her cutting edge?

- What have you learned about this student that you didn't know prior to this lesson? How will this affect your planning for his or her next lesson?

If you are familiar with guided practice and have been working with small guided practice groups in your classroom, you might be ready for a more challenging method of self-evaluation. During our Reading Recovery training, we had to videotape ourselves teaching a lesson and then write up a detailed evaluation of our teaching and the students' learning during that lesson. We found that we were our own best critics in this process. Videotape yourself teaching a guided reading lesson and ask yourself these questions:

- What do you notice about your teaching?

- Are you supporting students without making them dependent?

- Are the prompts you are using the most appropriate for your students' level of learning?

- How engaged are the students?

- Who is doing most of the talking during the lesson?

- What would you change or do differently another time?

CHAPTER 5

Planning for Independent Practice

My mother was very deliberate in instilling in us a love of books and the habit of reading. Summertime, especially, was a time to immerse us in books. Every June, as soon as school was dismissed, my family packed up and went to our cottage on Lake Winnipesaukee in New Hampshire. My mom ran the household and set up the daily schedule like a summer camp. This was necessary with 11 children to care for and keep busy. It was a matter of survival! We got up at a certain time each morning, did chores after breakfast and dinner every day, went swimming at appointed times, and had hours set aside to read after lunch and dinner every day (there was no TV in the house). Because we needed plenty of books for all that reading time, we visited the library in town once per week. My mom would take us all in the family station wagon and drop off the older bunch (all those in school) at the library while she and the "babies" went grocery shopping. The librarian set a limit of 10 books per person. An hour or two later, Mom would return to collect us and the 100 or so books we had checked out.

It was during these summer reading fests that I learned to love reading and appreciate what books could do for me. After lunch and dinner, my siblings and I would race to the living room to grab our favorite reading spot (the comfy, upholstered chairs were the favorites) and then settle into reading. Even the younger children who were not yet reading would sit and look at books or listen as one of the older children read to them. I remember my sister, Marge, who at preschool age would sit among the rest of us "reading" books by finding the word *we* systematically in all the books she had chosen. Since we were all close in age, we enjoyed many of the same books. Often there would be one book that would be particularly funny or engaging. One of us would be reading and laughing hysterically or would talk about the great book we were reading. So each of us would read not only the 10 or so books we had chosen but also many of the books our brothers and sisters had selected. My mother provided us with the basics for independent reading within an apprenticeship framework: a regular time for reading, access to books of our choice, and a built-in, supportive community of other readers. With these early experiences, we all developed into lifelong readers and book lovers.

— Ann

Too often, we work with students who are not illiterate; they simply aren't interested in books. These students can read (even those labeled as "below grade level"), but they choose not to spend time doing so. They have never experienced the joys of being lost in a book or the challenges of sharing what they have read to influence or entertain others. Like inexperienced or out-of-condition runners, these students lack stamina and can read with focus for only short periods of time. On standardized tests, they give up midway through the testing session. As adults, they rarely pick up a book or do more than glance through a newspaper or magazine. As children, they may have had many good models and demonstrations of the joys of reading. They probably had adequate instruction and guidance in their reading as they went through grade school in the reading group, labeled as a "robin" or a "bluebird." But they never acquired the reading habit. Today, most of them pay lip service to the importance of reading to their children, though they rarely find the time to read themselves.

Independent Practice in the Classroom

What these readers lack is experience with the full apprenticeship model for effective learning. They never arrived at the point where they were reading independently while the teacher watched and provided specific support and encouragement when necessary. They never were given the opportunity to respond to the question "How's it going?" and then to receive either the acknowledgement or the coaching to help them get lost in a book.

Apprenticeship Model Chart

MODELING	SHARED PRACTICE	GUIDED PRACTICE	INDEPENDENT PRACTICE
Teacher doing; Students watching	Teacher doing; Students helping	Students doing; Teacher helping	Students doing; Teacher watching

The role of independent practice in the apprenticeship model.

We are not talking about a sustained silent reading period during which the teacher catches up on e-mails, phone calls, or paper grading. We are not talking about DEAR time (Drop Everything And Read), when the teacher is engrossed in the latest novel and unconcerned about the students who have learned to simply sit quietly for 20 minutes pretending to read.

We are talking about making the little changes that can make a big difference, a tipping point in literacy instruction. Ann's family story points the way. The four key elements to the success of her family's reading time are shown below:

1. **Time:** Ann's mother set aside a predictable daily time for reading. The children could plan their reading. They learned how to carry their reading lives in their minds from one day to the next.

2. **Access to books:** It was no small feat for Ann's mother to pack all her children into the station wagon and take them to the library each week. It would have been much easier for her to leave the little ones home in the charge of the older ones as she did her grocery shopping in peace. Instead, she made the conscious decision to take the crew to the library on a predictable basis.

3. **Choice of materials:** Ann's mother did not assign books or tell her children how many pages they had to read each day. She did not enforce a "no talking" rule that kept the children from sharing their book finds. In fact, she had them read in the same room to encourage sharing. That brings us to the last key element.

4. **Social context:** Ann's mother planned the right time in the day for some quiet reading. (Who doesn't want a bit of quiet and rest right after lunch?) She encouraged her children to sign up for books they wanted to read next, so they often read more than their allotted 10 books. The focus was on understanding and enjoying the books, not getting every word right. In fact, she encouraged the making of approximations in the reading process. The little ones enjoyed hearing a story, Marge received kudos for patiently finding the word *we* in the books she scanned, the younger readers could use synonyms or temporary pronunciations if they came to a word they didn't know, or they could ask a sibling for a quick pronunciation or definition, and all of the children could talk about ideas they didn't understand.

The environment that Ann's mother created foreshadows the model Nancie Atwell describes in *The Reading Zone*: "When children practice reading in a context that's kind—with books they love, teachers who understand reading, and systems devised to make a hard thing easier—they're more inclined to practice, remember, make sense of, get better at, and love reading." (Atwell, 2007, p. 37)

Independent reading time is the point where students are reading texts of their choice while the teacher periodically checks in with individual students, ready to provide assistance when a student cannot independently problem solve. The teacher systematically confers with each reader, making notes about what each student is reading and his or her reading behaviors. The teacher then carefully chooses prompts to support the child or helps the student make a better text selection. The teacher's role is variable. It may mean listening to one child read as you take an impromptu running record while kneeling beside his or her desk. You might be following up with a child from yesterday to see how the new book choice is working. Your interaction with a student might be as simple as asking, "How's it going?" and noting that the child appears to still be deeply immersed in her latest book binge. You may gather two or three students who all are having trouble keeping track of characters in their books for a quick mini-lesson. During independent reading, all students, gifted readers to emerging readers, receive individualized support. The teacher is also taking careful notes with an eye toward future guided reading sessions and reading strategies for future review.

If we want to start a literacy epidemic, we need to find the tipping point so our students change from those who simply can read to those who read avidly. All of our teaching has led to this moment. Have our students caught the literacy epidemic? Can they read on their own? Do they look forward to opportunities to read? If not, how can we plan to bring them to this literacy tipping point?

What is the Tipping Point in Independent Practice?

We return to the roles of messenger, message, and context as the three critical factors to create a tipping point for change. As teachers, we are the primary messenger as maven, connector, and salesperson. As mavens, we know a range of children's and adolescent literature so that we can recommend great books for independent reading. As connectors, we understand that readability is more than a simple grade-level distinction on the computerized reading achievement test. An interesting topic coupled with a well-written, attractive text enables a child to read a book that would be too difficult under other circumstances. We connect a child with a just right book, one that's interesting and challenging without being overwhelming. As salespeople, we do book talks and share titles in ways that will entice even our most reluctant readers. (Debbie remembers very clearly her junior high teacher who would hand her a book from deep in his book closet with the words, "Your mother might not approve of your reading such a sensitive book." Debbie devoured each book the teacher suggested and felt very sophisticated.)

Our message during independent reading is a powerful one: reading is pleasurable, more pleasurable in fact than many of the competing ways to spend our time. To make this message "sticky," we need to make it personal and practical. Book choices are key to making independent reading personal. The book selection may also be very practical to the social needs of the children. Remember the midnight parties introducing the latest Harry Potter book and the following days when children sat with their noses in the book to find out what happened? Anyone not reading the book was left out of the social scene. (Debbie's daughter was at an art-oriented summer camp when one of the books came out. Parents preordered the book so the teens would have it as soon as it was available. The counselors allowed time in the schedule for the kids to read. When the famous violinist Joshua Bell visited the campus, the teens swarmed him for his autograph, but all they had with them to sign were their Harry Potter books. Some future historian will puzzle over the connection between the young violinist and the boy wizard as researchers examine the artifacts from that year!) Books often provide children with access to a social network of likeminded readers who are anxious to discuss the latest hot topic. Most important, though, is the simple enjoyment that comes from reading a good book. A reader who gets lost in a book is forever changed.

Finally, the context does matter. Readers will have difficulty getting lost in a book if they do not have extended time to read or the conditions that allow them to focus on their reading. These contextual factors can be narrowed to four key elements we discussed earlier in the chapter: time, access to books, choice of materials, and the social context.

Time

With the limited hours in the school day, we must make thoughtful decisions about how our students spend that time. The single most important activity in fostering students' growth in reading is *reading*—sustained, uninterrupted time engaged with text. Student achievement on standardized tests is directly related to how much time the test takers have spent reading (Allington, 2001; Krashen, 1993; Anderson, 1988; Taylor, 2000; Guthrie, 2002). Independent reading provides students with the opportunity to apply and practice their reading skills. As with the acquisition of any new skill, practice is an essential element in becoming a proficient, critical reader. When students spend extended time reading, they do the following:

- Increase comprehension
- Expand their vocabulary
- Become more fluent
- Experience a variety of genres
- Observe different authors' writing styles
- Learn about the world
- Increase their desire to read other books

More important than high scores on tests is that, when independent reading is a regular and treasured part of the classroom schedule, children develop the desire to spend time reading and the lifelong habit of reading. Joyful experiences with books translate into students who choose to read on their own both inside and outside of the classroom.

Ann's mother had an ironclad schedule for reading time after lunch. She knew readers need frequent, predictable times to dip into their reading in order to sustain interest. A musician who sits down at the piano to practice only once between lessons or with days between practices cannot improve. A person who wants to prepare for a mini-marathon cannot skip days or weeks of conditioning. A reader who wants to build interest and fluency has to read on a predictable, frequent basis.

Setting aside time for students to read books they have chosen for themselves not only facilitates their becoming more skillful readers but helps them develop into engaged, habitual readers as well. We want them to develop the habit of lifelong reading and to discover early on what Nancie Atwell calls "the reading zone": that place where passionate readers go when they're completely immersed in a book.

Here are some suggestions for setting up time for independent reading in your classroom:

- Make it a routine for students to come in, get their current independent reading book, and start reading at the start of the day or class period. (You will not miss grading the bell work or warm-ups that are often part of the beginning-of-class routine.)

- Block out a portion of the instructional time allocated for reading instruction each day for independent reading.

- In a self-contained classroom, dedicate the half hour after lunch or recess to independent reading.

- In a departmentalized setting, make 15 minutes on Tuesday and Friday "free reading" times, no matter what.

When students see that this time is held sacred, consistently set aside, and jealously guarded for independent reading, they will begin to plan for it and count on it.

Access to Books

I once heard the analogy made that the classroom library is the appetizer, and the library is the feast. As a classroom teacher, you want to entice with your classroom library while making the feast available through periodically scheduled trips to the school library. Any books housed within your classroom for independent reading need to be organized so that students can find the books they want and then find them again the next day. Here are some tips for doing that:

- Have students help you organize your classroom library, so they know where things are kept and how to put the books back. Clearly labeled shelves (for older students) or bins (for younger students) are a necessity. Reserve some books from the school library to add to the classroom collection throughout the year or treat your class to new books periodically, using bonus points from one of the book clubs. (Recently, Ann was helping to organize a classroom library by having students sort fiction from nonfiction and then the variety of types of fiction and nonfiction into separate baskets. She noticed some students were stacking a few books on their desks. When Ann asked them what these books were for, they responded, "Oh, these are some books I want to read!")

- Have a place for students to store their books between reading sessions. Some teachers encourage students to create their own bookmarks to identify the books they are reading. One of your class's early mini-lessons on independent reading must be on courtesy; for example, if there is only one copy of a book and someone else is reading it, sign your name on the reservation list, *and wait your turn.*

- Take weekly trips to the school library. Schedule regular book talks and lessons on choosing a book by the librarian. Keep a notebook with a photocopy of the cover of all the books you've read aloud so kids who are stuck when looking for a book can find one they liked or find an author they liked. Make sure students know where things are in the library. It can be an overwhelming place. Before you go, have students tell you their plans for finding their books, so they aren't milling around aimlessly in the library.

- Work with the school librarian to put together crates of reading materials across content areas with a variety of reading levels and topics appealing to your students' developmental levels. The crates could circulate to a new classroom each month to freshen up each classroom library.

- Set up books related by theme or topic, or text sets, that you introduce based on a favorite read-aloud or unit of study. Debbie has an ever-expanding collection of Joe Louis books and articles because of David Adler's biography of the fighter (see the Chapter 2 follow-up for using Adler's book as a read-aloud modeling lesson). She has text sets on Marian Anderson, the Japanese internment, Eastern European immigration, the Civil War, and astronomy. (Her college students refer to these as her "book binges" rather than her text sets.)

- Set up author collections. Again, Debbie's students have access to everything written by Allan Say and Jon Scieszka or illustrated by Lane Smith or Brian Selznick. We won't even begin to talk about her collection of Robert Sabuda pop-ups. Her enthusiasm is contagious, though. (Remember the role of the messenger in *The Tipping Point*?) Few of her college students leave her classes without going on author binges of their own.

- Buy a yearly subscription to a student periodical such as *National Geographic Explorer* or *Time for Kids*. If your school doesn't have the money for individual subscriptions, buy the minimum number of subscriptions allowed (usually 10). Don't send them home with students. After the periodicals have served as current reading material, file them by topic. That way, you'll be able to add material to your classroom library that is coordinated with the topics you are teaching. Pull out the issue on volcanoes when you are studying them in science. Even if the issue is a couple of years old, it will still be interesting reading.

- Expand your own knowledge of available books. Make friends with the librarian in the young adult and children's section of your public library or the owner of a children's bookstore. Subscribe to Web sites that feature new children's or adolescent literature, such as Carol Hurst's children's literature Web site (www.carolhurst.com), Jim Burke's English Companion Web site (http://englishcompanion.com), and the book lists offered by Nancie Atwell's students (http://www.c-t-l.org/kids_recommend.html). Use your professional memberships in the International Reading Association or the National Council of Teachers of English to find book reviews and other professional communities for teachers at your level. A big challenge for teachers is keeping up with all the books that are available to your students. No one expects us to have read every book in our classroom library, but we do need to be well acquainted with the books our students are reading. Where do we find the time to get this done? As usual, you'll have to be creative and make the most of "stolen" time. Ann reads kids' books as a treat, enjoying them as light bedtime reading. Debbie reads at the breakfast table while her teenagers are still sleeping. Her teens think it's a real treat when Debbie declares it a "book night" at the supper table so everyone may read while they eat.

- Keeping books in the car is a good way to grab some moments to read while you're stuck in traffic or waiting for someone. Keep books in your backpack or purse to read during down time whenever you are on the go. If you own a Kindle or other electronic reader, include young adult titles in your virtual collection. Establish family times to read and discuss books. If evenings are too busy or if everyone is too tired at that time of day, try family breakfast book time or any time during the day when everyone is together. Teachers can team up to read and share their thoughts about books to save time. An easy way to do this is to record on a sticky note anything about the book that would be helpful for a teacher to know when planning lessons or conferring with students—i.e., comprehension strategies, challenging vocabulary, theme, other pertinent story elements, and so on.

Choice of Materials

We have worked with school administrators and parents who insist that the only way to raise test scores is through a steady diet of challenging books. Computer systems track students' reading choices and their scores on the follow-up tests. Students are allowed to select books only in their test-determined level. Picture books earn a half point or are not counted by school programs. The goal for students ends up being the accumulation of points for a pizza party, not the enjoyment of the books themselves. Too many schools punish students for not accumulating enough points by taking away recess or even physical education classes. The students are robbed of the joy of reading and left with only the drudgery of doing it.

Here are some ways to encourage choice in independent reading that will help your readers build fluency and stamina while enjoying the reading experience.

- Make sure students have access to books and magazines representing a variety of reading levels and topics.

- Use books from different reading levels and topics in your read-alouds. Model thinking strategies with easy materials and encourage students to practice them at first on easier materials.

- Encourage students to read for fun. This could mean rereading favorite books or ones you've shared as read-alouds or in guided reading. This also means encouraging picture books, not just chapter books, for developing readers.

- Have students keep a list of everything they've read, so they can see their progress. Ask them to note trends in their reading. Have they found a genre or author they enjoy? Are there similar books they could try? Notice and celebrate the amount they've read, not with prizes or gimmicks, but with your attention.

- Invite students to evaluate books for other readers. They can chart the books the class has read and use color-coded dots to indicate their level of enjoyment. (Ann likes the stoplight metaphor: green is a "go" for everyone; yellow is a "caution" because only some would enjoy it; red is a "stop" because it isn't worth the time.)

- Have periodic sharing times when students can discuss the books they've enjoyed. Use the metaphor of the shopping cart from Web sites and tell students to put the title of a book they want to read in their carts.

It is important to remember that the students' reading should be primarily at their independent reading level (95%+ accuracy, 90%+ comprehension) in order to build fluency and stamina. Don't confuse books used in guided reading when you are there to provide assistance with books for independent practice. Challenge the fuzzy thinking that dictates that students should practice on material that is far too difficult for them. Using a sports analogy, independent reading practice is the daily training run, not the marathon. The daily training runs have to be done before any marathon can be successfully attempted.

Social Context

Students can be the best salespersons for each other. Have them make recommendations about books to other students. When interests are a topic of discussion in group meetings, students learn about each other and begin to make connections between books they have read and classmates who would enjoy reading those books. Who can resist taking a look at a book that a peer has offered to us by saying, "I've read this book, and knowing what you like, I think you'd really enjoy reading it." Consider the effect the Harry Potter or Stephanie Meyers's Twilight series have had on developing readers. Recommendations from adolescent to adolescent made those books popular and spread their popularity to younger and older readers.

You can establish a supportive, social atmosphere in your classroom. This is important, of course, throughout the school day, but it is especially important for independent practice.

- Set up and regularly review and practice routines for getting a book, returning a book, saving a book, and keeping a log of one's own reading.

- Set up procedures for sharing favorite reading spots.

- Set up procedures so students can ask for assistance without disturbing other readers.

- Model reading and enjoying books of different genres and difficulty levels yourself. Encourage students to pick books at an easy reading level by showing how you, and most adults, spend 80% or more of your reading time with easy-to-read, enjoyable material and no more than 20% of that time reading challenging materials.

- Model the kind of comments and observations you want your students to share with their classmates. Talk about the power of words and tone to help or hurt people. Model positive ways to address issues. Post a chart of words or phrases that will help make the class run smoothly. ("Please," "Thank you," and "I'm sorry" need to be at the top of the list!) Do not allow any teasing about the books anyone chooses or the levels of reading anyone pursues.

- Have a repertoire of ways in which students can share their independent reading. These may include turn-and-talk, charts on the wall, sticky notes in a book, formal book presentations every grading period, times for readers of similar books to get together and share, student-made book displays, recorded commercials, and student-authored book reviews. The possibilities are endless, but they do need to be taught and sequenced based on your students' prior experiences.

- Set regular and predictable times for sharing in partners or small groups. Small-group discussions can be structured similar to adult book groups.

- Establish a chart of class experts. You want students to be able to look at the chart and recommend book experts to each other: "If you want a good mystery, talk to Sarah. If you love to read about the history of the Civil War, see Beth. If you want to read about astronomy, see Jack." As a teacher, strive to notice and name areas of expertise so every student has a specialty.

A Note From Debbie

Emotional issues can interfere with a reader's ability to focus on and respond to books during independent practice time. I found myself unable to read for enjoyment for a long period of time after my husband's death. I finally took Regie Routman's advice and kept a reading journal. I made myself read young adolescent novels, reading a few more pages each day while maintaining focus. When I finished a book, I wrote its title and a short synopsis of it in a special notebook. I read over 20 of those books before I was able to read a novel written for adults, and then I started with fluff mysteries. If I had to read that many "easy" books and chart my progress to build my focus and stamina, I cannot be surprised that some of my struggling readers have to read and chart many, many easy books before gaining confidence in themselves as readers.

A Note From Ann

Certainly, the teacher sets the tone for the classroom environment. Despite the fact that any group of students includes high-level readers, those who struggle, and those who are somewhere between these extremes, everyone has the right to enjoy reading books that he or she chooses. In an adult book club, all readers are welcome, regardless of their level of skill as a reader. We have often noted that those students who struggle with the process of reading often have the most thoughtful responses to text. We try to keep Marie Clay's caution to Reading Recovery teachers in mind: Do not make assumptions about students: they may turn out to be wrong. (Clay, 1993b)

Planning Frames for Independent Practice Time

Yes—planning for successful independent practice time takes some effort. It is not enough to attend to the time, access to materials, freedom of choice, and social context. We can't simply say, "Drop everything and read" and expect all students to become engaged. In the independent phase of the apprenticeship model, the students are *doing* while the teacher is *watching*. Irene Fountas and Gay Su Pinnell (2001), Regie Routman (2003), and Nancie Atwell (2007) make clear distinctions between independent reading and sustained silent reading (SSR). These authors have identified the following characteristics to distinguish independent reading from SSR:

- Time for reading independently is an integral part of the reading block or workshop.

- Teachers continue to support students' reading through instruction via mini-lessons, individual conferences, written communications, and group sharing.

- Teachers and students give book talks to provide information about and pique interest in books.

- Teachers guide students to choose books that are just right for them.

- Students spend more time reading.

- Students keep a record of what they read.

- Students reflect on their reading and write about texts they are reading.

- Teachers monitor students' progress through observation and record keeping.

In the modeling phase of the apprenticeship model, the teacher is explicit in the demonstrations, using precise language to highlight the thinking involved in the task. In the shared practice phase of the apprenticeship model, as students focus on a new skill or strategy, they notice and name what the teacher is doing, predict what the teacher will do next, and then monitor the teacher's success. In the guided practice phase, the teacher notices and names, predicts, and monitors students' use of the targeted skill or strategy. Now, in this final phase of independent practice, the teacher notes if students can notice and name what they are doing (using metacognitive thinking), if they can predict what they need to do next to be successful, and if they are self-monitoring and making adjustments. The teacher also notes if a targeted skill or strategy has become so familiar to students that it has moved to an unconscious level, surfacing only when there is difficulty. The teacher notes how students respond to new levels of difficulty and decides what to do next instructionally: Does the whole apprenticeship cycle need to be repeated, or can the teacher simply move back to shared practice or guided practice?

Let's look at an example.

Example From a Fifth-Grade Class

A group of students in a fifth-grade class are hooked on Margaret Peterson Haddix's Shadow Children series. These students eagerly read and talk about the books in the series. Listening in, however, the teacher realizes that the students are having difficulty keeping track of the story across the novels. At this point, she decides to call a book group together to provide specific instruction on ways to keep track of a complicated plot and multiple characters. She invites the students to participate in the group and sets a time for the group to meet. This allows students to finish the reading they have planned and prepare for the appointment. During the session together, the teacher makes a connection between the story maps students have used on simpler texts and how the maps might be used with these more complex texts. The teacher does not have to model again. She can refer to the modeling done earlier and move to the shared and guided phases of instruction. With the students' assistance, the teacher maps the connections between the first two novels and assists the students as they work together to map the connections between those novels and the third book in the series. They then continue with their reading. The teacher writes a quick summary of the small-group lesson in her notebook and then makes an appointment on her planning calendar to check back with the group in three or four days to see if these students are now able to make the connections among the novels independently. The teacher might note that she could challenge the students to try their new understanding with another series of parallel novels, such as Lois Lowry's *The Giver, Gathering Blue,* and *The Messenger,* once they have finished the Haddix series.

Using the Planning Frame

Our planning framework for independent practice follows the before, during, and after reading framework we've used in previous chapters.

✔ BEFORE READING

- First, are the conditions for effective independent reading instruction in place? Have you addressed time, materials, choice, and context? If so, you can now make your daily plan.

- Is there a particular skill or strategy you want to highlight for the whole group before students begin reading? This is not initial teaching, but a reminder of what they have already seen modeled and practiced.

- Is there a content area-connection you can make by highlighting particular texts? For example, is a new *National Geographic Explorer* available? Have you set up a Joe Louis text set? You can do a quick commercial: "If you were fascinated by the story of Lincoln's boyhood here in Indiana, you'll really enjoy reading this book, *Abe Lincoln: The Boy Who Loved Books*."

- How will you have students communicate their plans for the time period? Will you note student responses on a grid as you do a quick roll call to learn who is choosing a new book, who is starting a new book, who is continuing to read, who is finishing one? Will you have a sign-up sheet for those who are looking for or trying out a new book, so you can provide assistance if necessary? Do students have their reading logs to track their book choices and reading progress?

- Which students will you target for your observations today? This is a time for individual conferences and informal reading assessments based on a student's book choice. At the lower grades, you might have three or four students to whom you provide encouragement by checking in daily and confirming that they are reading at their independent reading level. For others who can sustain the independent practice time, you won't need to offer your specific support for two or three reading sessions at a time. At least once a week, most children want the teacher's attention, even if they do not need it. A rule of thumb is to plan on meeting with at least two students a day for an in-depth conference (five or six minutes). That way, you'll have monitored each student's independent reading at least twice during a six-week grading period. At the upper grades, you'll want to meet with individuals a minimum of two times a grading period. The notes you've taken about individuals together with their reading logs will provide the data you need if you must assign grades for this independent practice time.

- What routines and procedures will you use to encourage student sharing? When will that sharing time occur? (Remember, it needs to be frequent and predictable so students can make the best use of their time, and yours.)

- Plan how you will use your time when students are reading independently. Be sure to make any instruction or review of procedures before the independent reading time brief and to the point.

✔ DURING READING

- Keep your teacher notebook with you as you observe individuals, confer with selected students, and observe general issues affecting all the students.

- Meet with one small group (two or three students is a good size) for specific skill or strategy instruction and support. Keep this instructional time to no more than 10 minutes.

- Look for cross-curricular connections in students' reading that can be highlighted and shared with the whole group during the sharing time at the end of independent practice time.

- Find one reading strategy you have noticed students using and highlight that strategy by naming it at the close of the reading time. If you honor good thinking by noticing and naming it, students will be more likely to pay attention to it themselves. Students notice what they think the teacher values. Use that to your advantage by noticing and naming actions you want to encourage.

Study buddies share their thoughts

A Note From Debbie

I found a planning and record-keeping system for conferences on the Choice Literacy Web site (www.choiceliteracy.com) that has made my teaching life so much easier. The teachers featured on the site, Gail Boushey and Joan Moser, recommend using a three-ring binder divided into sections. My adaptation of their conferring notebook for this independent practice time includes a calendar in the first section so I can quickly make appointments with students and remember to come back to them during the independent practice time on another day, as I had promised. The next section is an alphabetical chart of my students written on grid paper. I write down the date next to the child's name each time I confer with him or her during independent practice time. That way, I make sure I don't overlook someone. In the third section of the binder, I have a page for each child so I can make notes about individual interests, the results of running records, ideas for new books, specific instructional needs, etc. In the fourth section, I write down skill or strategy mini-lessons that students need, and then I write individual's names down under the mini-lessons. In that way, I can easily schedule small groups whose membership changes based on skill level or need for strategy review. In the fifth section, I jot down topics for mini-lessons that the whole class seems to need, connections I want to make to curricular topics, or ideas for books I want to share. After each session, I go back to the calendar and jot down which strategy I highlighted during the introduction and/or debriefing, which student's thinking I noticed and named, or which curricular connection or book recommendation I made. This serves as a record of what we've accomplished as a class during these sessions.

✔ AFTER READING

- Invite students to notice and name what went well for them in their reading as well as any difficulties. What predictions did they make regarding content (e.g., What will happen next, or what do they expect to learn next?) and the processes they'll use to deepen their comprehension? Invite them to self-monitor their effectiveness as readers at this time.

- Have students evaluate how well the procedures went during independent reading time. Was it quiet enough? Were there any difficulties getting or returning the books? What went well? What are possible solutions to problems in the classroom-management aspects of this independent practice time?

- Provide time for students to simply talk with a buddy about the book they are reading.

- Use your notes to decide what is needed next for instruction. Which students need support? Would that support be best provided in guided reading or is this a new skill or strategy that would be best addressed by moving through the entire apprenticeship model?

- What specific instruction would benefit the whole class? What would be the most effective and efficient way to provide that instruction using the apprenticeship model?

- Then, most important, assess for your big-picture goals. Are students becoming more capable and independent readers? How do you know?

Echoes Across the Curriculum

You should always have a range of reading materials from very easy to very challenging available for students. Your collection should include picture books (especially the extended ones that introduce an era or difficult topic), novels, and biographies, as well as news or science magazines, reference books, and other nonfiction texts. To increase your effectiveness in teaching social studies, history, health, science, or any other content area, make sure your classroom library and the books borrowed from your school library reflect the topics you study at your grade level. Students can read more on a topic you've introduced, or they might discover a brand-new topic. Either way, they expand their knowledge of that subject area.

To get the most power from this independent practice time, encourage students to make connections to their reading across content areas in school and at home. Help them highlight connections to content they've already learned. Guide them to become sensitive to the fact that once they've been introduced to an idea or fact, they can start seeing connections to it everywhere.

The same is true with vocabulary. Which words have they run across in their reading that are interesting or that hold a special connection to other areas of your instruction? Help students see and celebrate echoes from their reading lives across the day.

Change Over Time and Across Developmental Levels

Beginning in kindergarten, independent reading must be a part of the daily schedule in all classrooms. Carve an appropriate amount of uninterrupted time out of your busy classroom schedule to allow students to just read. Students will not be able to spend extended periods of time reading right away, however. Just as a runner doesn't start with a marathon, a reader won't successfully start with an hour of silent reading.

Based on the experiences of Jeff Williams, literacy coach for the Solon City, Ohio, school system, the table below lists suggestions for the amount of time to allocate to independent reading.

GRADE LEVEL	BEGINNING OF YEAR	END OF YEAR
Kindergarten	5–10 minutes	15–20 minutes
Grades 1–2	15–20 minutes	20–25 minutes
Grades 3–5	20–40 minutes	40–50 minutes
Grades 6–8 (non-departmentalized)	30–45 minutes	45–60 minutes

Possible Solutions to Behavioral and Management Issues

Before assuming that any management issues are the result of your students' behaviors, check your own planning. Are routines and procedures in place so students know what is expected of them? Do they know how to solve routine problems? Have you put the four key components in place: a predictable time, a range of interesting materials, student choice, and a supportive social context?

Of course, students have roles and responsibilities during independent reading. First, they have to behave in ways that do not interfere with other learners. Students need to learn to pick books that are just right for them to read and enjoy independently. Keeping a record of books is a way for students to see what they have accomplished and to share this information with their teacher and parents.

To help both you and your students make the transition to this quieter time of the school day, review your routines and procedures for independent practice time and then focus on the act of reading itself. We can talk to students about warming up to a book as they prepare to get into the "reading zone." They learn to re-engage with a book they have been reading by observing what we do when we are reading aloud to them—we review what we have read so far, perhaps reading the last page or paragraph in the previous chapter, and we recall the questions we had and the predictions we made when we last read the book. We can make the analogy to swimming—most of us don't just dive in, especially if the water is cool. We give ourselves time to slowly become accustomed to the water temperature, entering gradually before diving in. Another analogy is that of runners warming up their muscles and stretching before hitting the road.

Some students refuse to either dip into our reading pool or jog along our reading route. These students may need some specific instruction and support as they learn to focus during independent reading time. The chart on page 138 shows several mini-lessons that address impediments to a student's ability to focus during independent reading time.

Some students need additional support to even realize they should enjoy independent reading time. Here are some additional supports for these students:

- Use audiobooks. Well-dramatized, well-read audiobooks will transport a listener. Don't relegate the audiobooks for use only by your problem students. They are a benefit for readers of all levels. (Debbie has a subscription to www.audible.com so she can also indulge in well-read audiobooks!)

- Encourage students to read with a buddy. Teach them when and how to consult with one another at the end of a predetermined section to talk about what they've read and clarify understandings.

- If necessary, allow younger readers to "whisper read" alone or with a partner until they can read silently with understanding.

- Encourage sketching or the use of graphic organizers to help students make sense of what they are reading or hearing. Stop frequently and help students monitor their attention.

- Have students estimate how many paragraphs they can read in a focused way and then put a dot at the end of that paragraph. Tell them to read to the dot and then monitor themselves for understanding.

- Keep track of the length of time a student can read in a focused way. Have the student keep a private chart of his or her individual success in increasing reading stamina. It's not enough to sit still for longer periods of time. We're talking about reading with understanding for longer periods of time.

To Sum it Up

We are the mavens, the connectors, and the salespeople of the literacy epidemic. We impart the most important message to our students: *reading is enjoyable.* Our role as messenger during this independent reading time, our choice of engaging and accessible reading materials to make our message "sticky," and our establishment of a supportive social context, will help our students reach a literacy tipping point in our classrooms. We experience yet another benefit through the independent reading phase. As we help students take charge of their own reading, we will find ourselves talking with them reader to reader. We will bond with them through our book discussions. We will know them as individuals, and they will come to know us as people through our love of books. We will have, at the end of the school year, a room full of students who not only can read but who do read.

	K–2	3–5 (INCLUDING THE PREVIOUS COLUMNS)	6–8 (INCLUDING THE PREVIOUS COLUMNS)
BEFORE: MINI-LESSONS	• Learning what independent reading looks like and sounds like • Selecting books and returning them to the classroom library • Handling books respectfully to keep them in good shape for everyone to enjoy • Finding books in classroom library • Using different kinds of information to select books: - front cover -interesting illustrations or pictures -favorite authors -friends' and teachers' recommendations -books read aloud by the teacher -favorite books -sequels to a favorite books -book lists • Choosing just right books • Thinking about what they are reading • Talking about what they read with a partner or small group • Coming back to attend to the teacher after "buzzing" with a partner or small group	• Choosing just right books • Self-monitoring for comprehension during silent reading • When to abandon a book • Ways to keep a record of books read • Identifying fiction and nonfiction text • How to read new genres • Ways to "warm up" to a book • Writing responses to text • Giving a book talk • Creating a list of books to be read • Using context to problem solve words and/or determine meaning	• Comprehending over extended periods of time when reading "big, fat books" • Choosing new types of books and periodicals • Choosing between challenging YA (Young Adult) literature and popular adult literature • Reading current news periodicals, science journals, and so on, targeted to an adult audience • Looking for bias in an author's stance • Using Internet search engines to find appropriate reading materials
DURING: CONFERRING PROMPTS	• How is it going? • What are your favorite parts? • What is a place that begs to be read out loud? • Would you read this page for me? (The teacher can then do a quick assessment of oral reading and decoding strategies.)	• How is it going? • How do you decide whether to keep reading a book? • How do you decide what to read next? • What are you picturing as you read? • What does this remind you of from our class? • Who else in class might enjoy this book? • How are you helping yourself focus? • Is there anything I can do to help?	• How is it going? • What do you think of the book up to where you are now reading? • Why did you choose this book? • Is the book engaging you? Why or why not? • What is the author's style? What do you think of this style? • Have you read books by this author before? How do they compare to this book? • What's happening? What questions do you have as you are reading? • How does the structure of this text differ from ones you read when you were younger?
AFTER: SHARING/BUZZING	• What is too good to miss? • What questions does this book raise? • What connections can we make to what we already know? • What would help us as readers? • Have we stayed focused as we shared? • Have we helped one another? • What could we do differently next time?	(See previous column.)	(See previous column.)

CHAPTER 5 FOLLOW-UP

A Closer Look at Planning Independent Practice

Because we have limited hours in the school day, we are forced to make decisions about how to make the best use of that time—for our students as well as ourselves. Engaging students in independent reading practice is the best use of their time. They will grow more as readers with more time spent immersed in a good book of their choice and less time spent on worksheets or other activities that require minimal reading (Allington, 2001). Moreover, the priorities we set in the classroom will directly affect the message we send to students. By devoting time to independent reading in the classroom schedule, we communicate to our students that reading is important. Finally, if we want students to develop the lifelong habit of reading, we need to cultivate and nurture that habit as they learn to read and read to learn.

Teachers may have to ease some students into independent reading by helping them choose engaging books they can read and spending time discussing books and supporting their reading. To help students spend the time productively, teachers plan for the four key elements to a successful independent reading time.

1. **Time:** There are frequent, predictable times for independent reading so students can anticipate the reading time and learn to carry their reading lives from one session to the next.

2. **Access to books:** Classroom libraries echo the themes and topics from the content areas being taught. The materials vary in genres and difficulty levels.

3. **Choice of materials:** Students choose reading materials that interest them. The materials are organized so they are easy to find each time a student needs them.

4. **Social Context:** Independent reading gives students something to talk about and share, as well as offering the individual child a way to bond with a teacher through conversations about books.

Here are resources to help you find ways to encourage your students as they build reading stamina and discover the enjoyment of being lost in a book.

Sources to Help Plan, Organize, and Use a Classroom Library During Independent Reading

The Reading Zone by Nancie Atwell

Guiding Readers and Writers, Grades 3–6 by Irene Fountas and Gay Su Pinnell

Reading Essentials by Regie Routman

Still Learning to Read by Frankie Sibberson and Karen Szymusiak

If you need more resources on finding books that engage readers, here are some Web sites to explore.

Web Sites for Finding Engaging Books for Students

www.scholastic.com
Scholastic is the go-to site for everything dealing with classroom libraries. Find lists of books for your students, links to authors, and professional books for yourself.

www.lrobb.com/web/guest/classroom_libraries
Laura Robb lists seven compelling ways that classroom libraries benefit your students.

www.readinga-z.com
This Web site offers downloadable, printable leveled books to bolster your classroom library and guided reading program. There is a subscription charge for a classroom or building, but it's well worth it to gain access to this indispensable source for classrooms located in remote or materials-poor areas.

http://hill.troy.k12.mi.us/staff/bnewingham/myweb3/library%20Organization.htm
If you need help organizing your classroom library, this is the place for you. See examples of how other teachers have organized their collections and even download labels. The list of authors is up-to-date with children's interests.

http://teachersmentor.com/readingk3/class_library.html
A retired teacher provides hints and tips for acquiring a classroom library and organizing it. The sections on making paperback books and ways to keep track of your books are very practical.

www.fountasandpinnellleveledbooks.com
This Web site provides instructional information about books organized by reading level, by an alphabetical list of titles, and by genres.

www.c-t-l.org/kids_recommend.html
Nancie Atwell's Center for Teaching and Learning Web site lists students' recommendations for best-loved books grouped by grade level. It's a great student-centered source for books.

www.trelease-on-reading.com/biblios.html
If you don't know Jim Trelease's *Read-Aloud Handbook*, this site will provide an introduction. You will also find in-depth reviews of books published since the last edition of the book. The books he recommends are wonderful for both read-alouds and independent reading.

www.guysread.com
Author Jon Scieszka keeps this site quirky and lively so that boys will want to come to it for book recommendations.

Time Management

If you have only a single block of time in which to teach reading or reading in combination with a content area, how do you make it all fit? One way to think of this block of time is as a cycle. This entire cycle might occur on a single day or might stretch across a couple of days. You want the modeling and shared practice to be fresh in students' minds, and you also want frequent opportunities for sharing and celebration, so a single cycle would probably stretch across no more than three days.

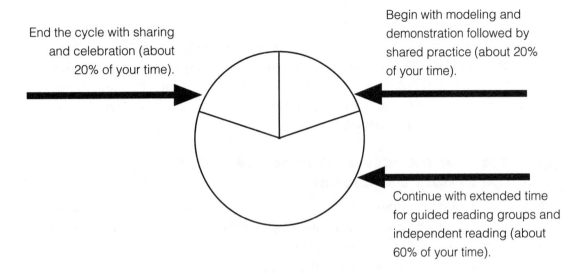

End the cycle with sharing and celebration (about 20% of your time).

Begin with modeling and demonstration followed by shared practice (about 20% of your time).

Continue with extended time for guided reading groups and independent reading (about 60% of your time).

What you focus on in your instruction may be initially dictated by your school's curriculum. Then your notes on your students will inform your instruction. You will see if the whole class needs instruction on finding a pronunciation for multisyllable words or ways to use context clues. You'll know if most of your students are having difficulty seeing connections or making inferences. You'll model the targeted skill or strategy, provide shared and guided practice in its use, and then coach students to use that skill or strategy during independent reading. You'll notice and celebrate students' growing control over that skill or strategy.

You may find yourself helping students apply a specific reading strategy on increasingly more difficult material, especially as you help students apply what they know about reading books they consider fun to more challenging materials in the content areas. Starting with a picture-book biography such as David Adler's *Joe Louis: America's Fighter*, you might move on to other picture book biographies of people from the 1920s and 1930s for guided and shared reading. On the next pass, your teaching points remain the same, but the difficulty of the texts increases, perhaps to the level found in your assigned social studies and literature textbooks. On yet another pass with the same teaching point, you might increase the level of difficulty to include resources from the library or from trade books focused on the time period. All the while, you will begin independent practice time by highlighting books and other materials in your classroom library related to the era you are studying. "If you thought Joe Louis's story was interesting, you might like to read about another fighter from that era, James J. Braddock. Here's an article about him from the PBS Web site." "What was it like to be a child during the Great Depression? Here's a section in our *We Were There, Too!* book by Phillip M. Hoose, or, if you can handle a very sad story written in an unusual way, here's the audiobook of *Out of the Dust* by Karen Hesse. I have copies of the book here, too, so you can follow along." As your students build their background information about the 1920s and '30s, they also learn how to remember and organize main ideas and details while reading.

You and your students are on a sort of journey together through the school year. Your content area and reading curricula set your course for you; some landmarks are represented by required assessments, and you have done your big-picture planning for your school year in advance.

Your students bring their individual strengths and needs. It's up to you to respond to the needs of your class as you sequence experiences and make the adjustments needed to sail smoothly in the most efficient and effective manner. Your planning for this independent practice cycle is critical. It is during this time that students learn to value the trip (the learning process) as well as the destination (the information learned). And, if all goes well, your students will arrive at that destination fired with the love of reading.

Sample Plan for Independent Practice in a Middle School Classroom

How does independent practice look in a classroom? In one of the middle schools in which Debbie works, the students are in a double-period English and reading class. Here's Debbie's lesson with those students incorporating independent practice.

There are 30 minutes for independent practice scheduled three times a week in this middle school English classroom. Most of the students are engaged in reading books of their choice or listening to an audiobook. I realize there are three students who have difficulty starting a new book. They return to ones they've read many times before, or they attempt multiple texts for independent reading only to abandon them. I can understand their reluctance. Starting a new book takes time and, especially in the case of a narrative, can be an emotional investment. I also have three students reading far below grade level. I want to see if their fluency has increased in the last two weeks. A new student moved in last week. She seems to be participating, but I'm not sure if she is really reading or simply faking it. I may not have time to reach all of them in one day, but I want to plan to meet with each student during the week.

Mentor Texts: Fiction and nonfiction texts about the Civil War

Key teaching point for reading: Proficient readers monitor their understanding as they read historical fiction and nonfiction by asking: "Does this make sense when I think about what I already know about the time period?"

Content Connections:

Social Studies: These students are studying the Civil War as part of a grade-level theme. They can build a network of background information through some of the texts available for independent reading.

Literature: Students are reading one of five classic novels about the Civil War as part of the grade-level theme: *Across Five Aprils* by Irene Hunt, *Soldier's Heart* by Gary Paulsen, *Rifles for Watie* by Harold Keith, *Bull Run* by Paul Fleischman, or *The Red Badge of Courage* by Stephen Crane.

Lesson Plan Outline

Management: Students know the procedures for independent reading time. Three students are assigned to put out the book baskets in six locations strategically scattered around the room to avoid traffic jams. Students can also read books they've checked out from the library or their book for English class. Each student has a reader's log stored in a basket by the cluster of desks so they are easy to distribute. A student is in charge of both distributing and collecting the books. The set-up work will be done after I do a book talk and remind students of a reading strategy. Students will put out the baskets and distribute the logs while I go through the roll, asking each student what he or she is working on. Options for work include: (1) continuing to read a particular title, (2) quietly discussing a text with a book buddy to begin the period, (3) writing a synopsis of some recently completed reading, and (4) searching for a new text. I use these numbers as a code on my record sheet. If I notice that a student has jumped titles frequently, is constantly searching for a new book, or chooses writing or discussing twice in a row, I offer quiet counsel or mark that student for an immediate conference. Students know that independent reading time will begin after I finish the roll call. My classroom is set up so that every student has a partner.

Setting a purpose: I point to our map of the United States and our ongoing K-W-L chart on the Civil War period as references for a brainteaser. Then I ask partners to assign themselves the number 1 or 2. Those who chose the number 1 have 30 seconds to predict what strategy the North might have used to defeat the South. After the time is up, I ask those who chose the number 2 to predict what strategy the South might have used to defeat the North. Then I ask them to test their predictions against the information shown in the DVD, *The Civil War in Four Minutes*. The audio is a medley of Civil War tunes, and the graphic consists of a map of the United States from 1860. As a timeline scrolls from left to right at the bottom of the screen, one second equaling one week, the map changes colors as Southern states secede. Explosions on the map signify battles as they occur. The boundary lines between the Union and the Confederacy ebb and flow as battles are won and lost. All the while, a counter clicks in the right-hand corner of the screen showing the casualties for each side. It is a powerful video. I give students one minute to discuss ways in which what they just viewed related to their predictions.

Then I launch into my sales pitch: "Proficient readers always make connections between what they are reading and what they already know. They are constantly asking themselves, 'Does this make sense with what I already know?'

"If you are reading one of the Civil War books for English class, ask yourself when it takes place on this timeline. Can you see what military strategy is being used by either the North or the South? Can you see how that detail fits into what is happening in your novel?

"If you are interested in finding out more about what battles were like, you might be interested in some of the books in this basket. Here's *I'll Pass for Your Comrade: Women Soldiers in the Civil*

War by Anita Silvey, if you want to find out about some of the women who disguised themselves as men and fought in the war. *The Boys' War: Confederate and Union Soldiers Talk About the Civil War* by Jim Murphy is a good choice if you want to read interviews with the boys and teenagers who fought during the war. There are other books and articles of interest in there, too. Those of you who are reading *Bull Run* by Paul Fleischmann will be our experts on that battle.

"Whatever you read during the next 15 minutes, remember to ask yourself, Does this make sense with what I already know?

"I'll go through the roll call now. Helpers, please set out the baskets and pass out the reading logs. As soon as I've called your name and you've told me how you plan to use this time, please begin work."

✔ BEFORE READING

Students will be working independently. I have 15 minutes in which to check their progress, confer, and possibly call a small group together. Before they begin, I've determined which students I'll work with today and what I hope to accomplish with them.

✔ DURING READING

I take three minutes to help Chris choose between two Dorling Kindersley picture-packed reference books: *Civil War Battles and Leaders* and *Eyewitness: Civil War*. Because he is reading the Paul Fleischmann novel, I advise him to use the table of contents to find references to the Battle of Bull Run.

This leaves me 12 minutes. I kneel beside the new student, Janice, and ask "How's it going?" Her soft "okay" is not convincing. I notice she is reading *Across Five Aprils*, so I ask her to read me the page she is on. I take a running record. Janice makes only two minor miscues as she reads, but I notice that she is reading very quickly, overrunning the punctuation. Then I ask her to tell me about the book. "It's boring," Janice blurts. I know that most students find this to be a slow-moving book. Is that her difficulty, or is she having difficulty comprehending in general? I talk to her about books with slow beginnings and ask if she'd like to join a group that will be talking about strategies for dealing with slow beginnings. Janice nods, so I add her name to the group of three I identified earlier as needing help to get into new books. After I move away from her desk, I note after the running record that I want to assess Janice's comprehension soon. I put her name on the calendar for a time slot at the end of the week so I'll remember to get back to her.

Time has flown by, as usual. I have only a couple of minutes left. I spend 45 seconds with Victor, who responds to my "How's it going?" by showing me a section from the printed materials accompanying *The Civil War in Four Minutes,* saying that both those who were too wounded to return to battle and those who were killed were listed as casualties in the Civil War. Hmmmm. That changes our response to the numbers on the DVD at the beginning of class. I ask Victor to share this information with the whole class later. I spend another 45 seconds with Willy. He is slowly reading *Bull Run* for English class. When I ask him "How's it going?" he grins and says he likes how each person in the book has a couple of pages to give his idea of what is happening in the war. "I can read one of these each time we have independent reading and remember it pretty well," Willy offers. I celebrate his discovery of a format that works well for him and ask if maybe he could devise a way to remember each person by either drawing a thumbnail sketch or symbol for that person or writing a single word to sum up that person.

The allotted time is over.

✔ AFTER READING

The students groan when the timer goes off. I give them one minute to talk with their study buddy about what they've read. Today, I use a prompt that will narrow their responses: "Tell your buddy something you read today that connected with information you already knew. If there was something that didn't make sense based on what you already knew, tell your buddy that." I eavesdrop as best I can. When the minute is up, I ask for volunteers. After a couple of students share, I ask Victor to share the definition of the word *casualty* during the Civil War. I ask study buddies to tell each other how that information changes their understanding of the DVD we saw at the beginning of class. I pose the debriefing question for content: "Did you all learn something today about the Civil War?" Nods. Then I pose the debriefing question for process: "Did the independent reading procedures work so that you could all focus and read with understanding?" More nods. I know from eavesdropping that the students are aware of both what they've learned and how they've read. I don't need them to share this in a larger group. Then a hand is raised shyly: "We need more time to read."

I agree.

Echoes: Debriefing Process and Content

As readers, the students are becoming aware that their knowledge is a kind of mosaic. New pieces of information gleaned from both nonfiction and fiction sources help them visualize the Civil War period in United States history. If a new piece of information doesn't fit, as when we discovered the definition of *casualty*, we may have to look at the overall mosaic in a new way. As readers, we must constantly make and then check the new connections we are making.

Students have also expanded their background knowledge about the Civil War and shared their discoveries with others in the class. It will be easy for teachers of both English and social studies to draw upon this knowledge in their classes on the Civil War.

As a teacher, I have a better sense of my students as individual readers, but I, too, am left with questions and assumptions that must be checked. Because of the individual conferences, I can begin to learn more about the new student and her reading skills. I see that another student is beginning to notice his own progress as a reader. I have teaching points for future whole-class and small-group instruction. I have learned as much as my students have during this independent reading practice.

> ### *Your Turn*
>
> Regarding the tipping point:
> • In what ways did Debbie act as salesperson, maven, or connector in order to "sell" the lesson?
> • What was there in the social context to present independent reading time as desirable?
> Regarding the apprentice model:
> • In what ways were the students doing while Debbie was watching?

Trying it Out: An Invitation

Now it is your turn. Work with a colleague to map out classroom procedures that would support a calm and orderly use of independent reading time. Where would you store materials? How would you have students get their reading materials? How would you keep track of class work and the work of individuals? Ask your students: *What would help you focus as you read quietly in the classroom?* Work out some of your procedures with the students' help.

After you've put all aspects of the apprenticeship model in place, we offer you a second invitation. Take time to tell a story about you and your students as you've discovered the joys of reading together. Perhaps it will be similar to this account written by Ann after her work in a summer school setting:

I had the opportunity to teach a two-week summer class for fourth- and fifth-grade students who had not passed either the language arts or math portions of the state test. With only two weeks and four hours per day to work with the students, who read at a range of levels of proficiency, I realized that guided instruction for groups was not a possibility. I decided to set up a modified reading/writing workshop format for the class, including read-aloud, shared reading, and independent reading. I modeled how students could read aloud to their partner and discuss their books through the read-aloud I chose, The Tale of Desperaux *by Kate DiCamillo. The read-aloud did furnish the means for my modeling for students. Because the story of Desperaux was so engaging and rich, however, it gave us much more. The students loved the story and cheered on the little mouse as he dealt with overwhelming odds to show his love for the princess and to vindicate himself to his family and friends. My students and I bonded in this very brief time, largely through sharing this delightful tale.*

Our shared reading consisted of poems and related short stories. These provided material for our writing experiences. For independent reading, I assembled a classroom library organized by groups of levels that mirrored the reading abilities of the students in the class. I strategically partnered the students, pairing a stronger reader with a struggling reader so that everyone could spend time reading independently and then share books by discussing and rereading portions with a partner. One of the book bins contained traditional folk and fairy tales, as well as spin-offs, such as Jon Scieszka's The True Story of the Three Little Pigs, *for students who were hooked by* The Tale of Desperaux. *Students had a consistent time to read, access to books of interest to them, a choice of books, and a social context in which to read and share. The children's perceptions of reading changed.*

Even into the new school year, many of the students from that summer class would stop me in the hall or in the cafeteria and excitedly tell me what they were reading or that they were rereading The Tale of Desperaux *themselves. They borrowed books from my library and accepted my recommendations for related titles. Of course, I hoped this would translate into higher test scores for those students on the mandated tests. More important, I knew that the experience transformed the students into children who can and do read.*

Ann created a tipping point for her students, changing them from struggling readers to engaged readers. We hope that the ideas in this book help you create your own tipping point within your classrooms so that together we start a literacy epidemic.

References

Literature for Adults and Children Cited

Adler, D. (2005). *Joe Louis: America's fighter.* Orlando: Gulliver Books: Harcourt.

Anderson, L. H. (2002). *Thank you, Sarah.* NY: Simon & Schuster.

Boow, A. (2000). *Platypuses.* Bothell, WA: Wright Group/McGraw-Hill.

BRC Imagination Arts. (2005). Abraham Lincoln Presidential Museum. *The Civil War in four minutes.* DVD. Springfield, IL.

Brisson, P. (1998). *The summer my father was ten.* Honesdale, PA: Boyds Mills Press.

Civil War battles and leaders. (2004). NY: DK Publishing.

Cleary, B. (1983). *Dear Mr. Henshaw.* New York: HarperCollins Children's Books.

Connell, R. E. (1990). *The most dangerous game.* Mankato, MN: Creative Education.

Crane, S. (2009). *The red badge of courage.* New York: Puffin Books.

Creech, S. (2000). *The wanderer.* New York: HarperCollins Children's Books.

Delano, M. F. (2005). *Genius: A photobiography of Albert Einstein.* Washington, D. C.: National Geographic Society.

DiCamillo, K. (2004). *The tale of Desperaux* New York: Scholastic.

Dickens, C. (1847). *A Christmas carol.* NY: D. Dana Jr.

Eyewitness: Civil War. (2000). NY: DK Publishing.

Fleischman, P. (1993). *Bull Run.* NY: HarperCollins.

Freedom Writers. (1999). *The Freedom Writers diary.* New York: Broadway Books.

Garland, S. (1993). *The lotus seed.* San Diego: Harcourt Brace Jovanovich.

Haddix, M. P. Shadow Children series.

Hesse, K. (1997). *Out of the dust.* NY: Scholastic.

Hoose, P. M. (2001). *We were there, too!* NY: Farrar, Straus, and Giroux.

Hunt, I. (2002). *Across five Aprils.* New York: Berkley Publishing Group.

Jenkins, S. (2005). *Prehistoric actual size.* Boston: Houghton Mifflin.

Junior chronicle of the 20th century. (1997). NY: DK Publishing.

Keith, H. (1987). *Rifles for Watie.* New York: HarperCollins.

Kellogg, S. (1986). *Pecos Bill.* NY: Morrow.

Konigsburg, E.L. (1996). *The view from Saturday.* New York: Atheneum Books for Young Readers.

Korman, G. (2000). *No more dead dogs.* New York: Hyperion Books for Children, 2000.

Lowry, L. (1993). *The giver.* Boston: Houghton Mifflin.

Lowry, L. (2000). *Gathering blue.* Boston: Houghton Mifflin.

Lowry, L. (2004). *The messenger.* Boston: Houghton Mifflin.

Martin, B., Jr. & Archambault, J. (1989). *Chicka chicka boom boom.* NY: Simon & Schuster.

Murphy, J. (1990). *The boys' war: Confederate and Union soldiers talk about the Civil War.* New York: Houghton Mifflin.

Neuschwander, C. Sir Cumference series. Watertown, MA: Charlesbridge.

Parkes, B. (1998). *The sun.* Marlborough, MA: Newbridge.

Paulsen, G. (1998). *Soldier's heart.* New York: Dell Laurel-Leaf.

Polacco, P. (1994). *Pink and Say.* NY: Philomel.

Neufeld, D. (2002). *Wind power.* New York: Newbridge Educational Publishing.

Rawls, W. (1961). *Where the red fern grows.* New York: Bantam Books.

Ring, S. (2002). *Nature did it first.* Marlborough, MA: Newbridge.

Ryan, P. (2002). *When Marian sang.* New York: Scholastic.

Salisbury, G. (1994). *Under the blood red sun.* New York: Dell Yearling.

Say, A. (1993). *Grandfather's journey.* Boston: Houghton Mifflin.

Scieszka, J. The Time Warp Trio series

Scieszka, J. (1996). *The true story of the three little pigs.* New York: Puffin.

Silvey, A. (2008). *I'll pass for your comrade: Women soldiers in the Civil War.* New York: Clarion Books.

Simon, S. (1996). *The heart.* NY: Morrow.

Simon, S. (2006). *The brain: Our nervous system.* New York: HarperCollins.

Spiegelman, A. (2003). *The complete Maus.* London, England: Penguin.

Stanley, D. (1997). *Rumpelstiltskin's daughter.* NY: Morrow.

Winters, K. and Carpenter, N. (2003). *Abe Lincoln: The boy who loved books.* New York: Simon & Schuster.

West, J. (1945). *The friendly persuasion.* San Diego: Harcourt Brace Jovanovich.

White, E. B. (1952). *Charlotte's web.* New York: Scholastic, Inc.

Professional Literature Cited

Allington, R., & Walmsley, S. (Eds.) (2007). *No quick fix: The RTI edition.* New York: Teachers College Press, Columbia University.

Allington, R. (2001). *What really matters for struggling readers.* New York: Addison-Wesley Educational Publishers, Inc.

Anderson, R. C., Wilson, P., & Fielding, L. (1988). "Growth in reading and how children spend their time outside school." *Reading Research Quarterly, 23,* 285–303. Newark, DE.: International Reading Association.

Atwell, N. (2007). *The reading zone: How to help kids become skilled, passionate, habitual, critical readers.* New York: Scholastic.

Beaver, J. (2006). *Developmental reading assessment, K–3.* Parsippany, NJ: Pearson Education.

Beaver, J., & Carter, M. (2006). *Developmental reading assessment, 4–8.* Parsippany, NJ: Pearson Education.

Beers, K. (2003). *When kids can't read what teachers can do.* Portsmouth, NH.

Blanchard, K. & Johnson, S. (1982). *The one minute manager.* New York: William Morrow and Company.

Clay, M. (1991). *Becoming literate: The construction of inner control.* Portsmouth, NH: Heinemann.

Clay, M. (1993a). *An observation survey of early literacy achievement.* Portsmouth, NH: Heinemann.

Clay, M. (1993b). *Reading Recovery: A guidebook for teachers in training.* Portsmouth, NH: Heinemann.

Cunningham, P.M., & Cunningham, J.W. (1992). Making words: Enhancing the invented spelling-decoding connection. *Reading Teacher, 46,* 106–115.

Cunningham, P., & Allington, R. (2007). *Classrooms that work: They can all read and write.* Boston: Pearson Allyn and Bacon.

Diller, D. (2005). *Practice with purpose: Literacy work stations for grades 3–6.* Portland, Maine: Stenhouse Publishers.

Fountas, I., & Pinnell, G. (2001). *Guiding readers and writers grades 3–6.* Portsmouth, NH: Heinemann.

Fountas, I., & Pinnell, G. (2008). *Benchmark assessment system 1.* Portsmouth, NH: Heinemann.

Fountas, I., & Pinnell, G. (2008). *Benchmark assessment system 2.* Portsmouth, NH: Heinemann.

Gladwell, M. (2002). *The tipping point: How little things can make a big difference.* Boston, MA: Back Bay Books.

Guthrie, J. (2002). Preparing students for high-stakes test taking in reading. In A. Farstrup and S. Samuels (Eds.), *What research has to say about instruction* (pp. 370–391) Newark, Delaware: International Reading Association.

Harvey, S., & Goudvis, A. (2001). Tape 2. *Strategy instruction in action.* DVD. Portland, ME: Stenhouse Publishers.

Harvey, S., & Goudvis, A. (2007). *Strategies that work: Teaching comprehension for understanding and engagement,* 2nd edition. Portland, ME: Stenhouse Publishers.

Hoyt, L. (1999). *Revisit, reflect, retell: Strategies for improving reading comprehension.* Portsmouth, NH: Heinemann.

Hyde, A., Zemelman, S., & Daniels, H. (2005). *Best practice,* 3rd Edition. Portsmouth, NH: Heinemann.

Hyerle, D. (2000). *A field guide to using visual tools.* Alexandria, VA: Association for Supervision and Curriculum Development.

Johnston, P. (2004). *Choice words: How our language affects children's learning.* Portland, ME: Stenhouse Publishers.

Johnston, P. (2000). *Running records: A self-tutoring guide.* Portland, ME: Stenhouse Publishers.

Keene, E., & Zimmerman, S. (1997). *Mosaic of thought: Teaching comprehension in a reader's workshop.* Portsmouth, NH: Heinemann.

Krashen, S. (1993). *The power of reading: Insights from the research.* Englewood, Colorado: Libraries Unlimited, Inc.

Laminack, L., & Wadsworth, R. (2006). *Reading aloud across the curriculum: How to build bridges in language arts, math, science, and social studies.* Portsmouth, NH: Heinemann.

Pearl, N. (2007). *Book crush.* Seattle, Sasquatch Books.

Pederson, B. (2007). C.L.A.S.S.: Connected Learning Assures Successful Students. Retrieved April 19, 2008, from www.indianaclass.com.

Power, B. (2008, March 29). *Literacy spring cleaning.* Retrieved April 19, 2008, from http:www.choiceliterary.com/public/586.cfm

Reading Recovery of North America. (2008). *Sensitive observation of reading behavior, running record professional learning Package.* CD.

Rogoff, B. (1986). Adult assistance of children's learning. In T.E. Raphael (Ed.), *The contexts of school-based literacy* (pp. 27–40). New York: Random House.

Routman, R. (2003). *Reading essentials: The specifics you need to teach reading well.* Portsmouth, NH: Heinemann.

Routman, R. (2005). *Writing essentials: Raising expectations and results while simplifying teaching.* Portsmouth, NH: Heinemann.

Science and Children. (1963). Washington, D.C.: National Science Teachers Association.

Sibberson, F., & Szymusiak, K. (2003). *Still learning to read: Teaching students in grades 3–6.* Portland, ME: Stenhouse Publishers.

Smith, M. and Wilhelm, J. (2002). *Reading don't fix no Chevys.* Portsmouth, NH: Heinemann.

Smith, M. and Wilhelm, J. (2006). *Going with the flow: How to engage boys (and girls) in their literacy learning.* Portsmouth, NH: Heinemann.

Taylor, G., Pearson, D., Clark, K., & Walpole, S. (2000). *Beating the odds in teaching all children to read* (Report #2-006). East Lansing, MI: Center for Improving Early Reading Achievement (CIERA).

Trelease, J. (2006). *The read-aloud handbook.* NY: Penguin Books.

Tunnell M. and Jacobs, J. (2008). *Children's literature, briefly.* Upper Saddle River, NJ: Pearson Merrill Prentice Hall.

Vygotsky, L. S. (1962). *Thought and language* (E.H.G. Vakar, Trans.). Cambridge, MA: MIT Press.

Wilhelm, J. (2001). *Improving comprehension with think-aloud strategies.* New York: Scholastic.

Wilhelm, J. (2002). *Action strategies for deepening comprehension.* New York: Scholastic.

Appendix

Lesson Planning Frame

What is your main teaching point, the thing you want students to know or be able to do, no matter what, at the end of this lesson?

What aspects of the curriculum content knowledge and/or background knowledge covered in this lesson will students be able to apply toward other content areas?

Resources and materials:

BEFORE-READING ACTIVITIES: Hooking students' interest through modeling	
What I will do:	What my students will do:

DURING-READING ACTIVITIES: Shared practice to guided practice to independent practice	
What I will do:	What my students will do:

AFTER-READING ACTIVITIES: Clinching the lesson	
What I will do:	What my students will do:

TEACHER REFLECTION	
Did my students understand the teaching point? How do I know?	What connections and invitations did I extend to encourage independent reading in content areas?

A Glossary of "Desert Island" Teaching Techniques

These are called "desert island" strategies because they take little or no preparation and could be used if you found yourself teaching on a desert island.

Agenda as organizer: a brief written agenda to help students see the flow of the lesson.

Alphaboxes/alphachart: Using the alphabet as an organizer, students find a word to match each letter for a review or as an advanced organizer for a topic.

Anchor charts: The teacher and students together describe a process or define a term that is then posted so it can serve as a reference. Anchor charts remind students of the comprehension strategies they've been learning and why the strategies are useful.

Anticipation guides: Students respond in a variety of ways (agree/disagree; hand signals, ranking, etc.) to ideas that are key to the lesson. The activity's purpose is to generate curiosity and tap background knowledge and beliefs.

Attribute chart: Students list qualities such as "beautiful," "honest," "thoughtful," "cunning," and "smart" on a grid that allows a rating from 1–10. Then they work together to agree on a rating for each of those qualities for characters in the stories they are reading.

"Block party": Using cards with key ideas, lines of a poem, or key words, students mingle with other class members, sharing what is on their card and trying to put the clues together to identify what the topic will be.

Brace map: Students use David Hyerle's thinking map to analyze the component parts of physical objects.

Checklist for using strategies: After students have learned a comprehension strategy, they learn to monitor how they use that strategy with a checklist, e.g., Did I make connections to anything I've read before? Did I make connections to anything I've experienced? Did I search for connections?

Coding the text: Students use sticky notes (if they can't write in the books) to indicate where they have questions (?), responses (*), or connections (ooo). They use the coded sections in the follow-up discussion of the reading.

Cooperative learning roles: Students perform specific jobs when they are in a cooperative learning group, e.g., recorder, reader, summarizer, reporter, connector, illustrator, or encourager.

Cut-up stories (or schema stories): Students reconstruct a story that has been cut apart. Depending on where the cuts are made, the focus can be on organization, sequence, or fluency.

Debriefing process and product: When students work cooperatively, they should always monitor their success in working together as a group, think of ways to improve this process in the future, and see if they have learned or accomplished what they were assigned.

Definition poems: This is a patterned poem from Hoyt's *Revisit, Reflect, Retell.*

Draw something: Students make a drawing that depicts the literal meaning of what has happened so far in a story.

Exit cards: Students respond to prompts as they leave the classroom. Usually they write their responses on cards and hand them to the teacher. Prompts could be "Name one new thing you learned this class," or "Write down a question you have about . . ."

Flow chart for sequencing: This is one of David Hyerle's thinking maps, which allow students to sequence events in a story or steps in process.

Four-column organizer: (This could be any number of columns, depending on your purpose.) Students divide a sheet of paper into four columns and write the key idea in the first column. The next three columns depend on the teacher's purpose. For vocabulary, you might have the definition, the sentence in the book in which it was found, words related to the word's meaning (e.g., nation/national/nationalistic), and a memory aid for pronunciation.

FQR: A three-column organizer for facts, questions, and responses.

Frontloading information: Teaching key ideas and concepts before students encounter them in their reading.

Games for review: Bingo, Jeopardy, etc.

Glyphs: Using picture symbols to represent key information about a person or event.

Good angel/bad angel: Jeff Wilhelm's dramatization strategy to have students act out the pros and cons of a character's decision (2002).

Guided practice in pairs: After modeling a process, but before you have students use it independently, put students in pairs to help each other out as they try the new process.

"Hot seat" dramatization: Another dramatization from Jeff Wilhelm, in which a character is cross-examined about the motivations for his actions (2002).

Jigsawing: A cooperative learning activity in which a text is divided into chapters or sections. Groups of students are responsible for becoming experts on their section and then teaching it to the others.

Listing class "experts": Students who can help others are listed with their area of expertise. During workshop time, students can ask questions of these "experts" when the teacher is not available.

Making words: Pat Cunningham's game-like activity for building words from letters to help students see how words work. In addition to building the words, students sort the words, looking for patterns, and then use those patterns to spell new words.

Modeling/demonstration: Instead of simply telling students how to do something or giving directions, do the task yourself and talk through the process.

One-sentence summary: Students reduce a passage to a one-sentence summary to help them identify what is important and train themselves to remember it.

Pair/Share/Review: Students use this throughout a lesson at your invitation. They turn to their partner (pair), share what they've heard (share), and in this way rehearse and review the material.

Personal stories as examples: Students make connections with material more easily through a pertinent, personal story from a teacher with whom they have bonded.

Prediction riddles: These are teacher-written or student-written riddles that introduce vocabulary or a situation through a series of clues. The first clue is very broad. Each clue becomes more specific until the idea is clear.

Probable passages: Students sort a list of words with a partner into probable characters, settings, problems, and solutions. Then they write a "probable" story summary based on these predictions. As they read the real story from which the words were taken, partners see how closely their passage matches the story.

Props and pictures: Stories and nonfiction texts come alive with real objects, pictures, or photographs to help students picture situations.

Reciprocal teaching: Small groups of students take on the role of teacher to help the others make predictions, ask questions, look at vocabulary, and summarize the passage.

Read-alouds: The teacher reads the students a text in an engaging manner to provide background information, elicit an emotional connection to the upcoming subject, or to pose questions.

Real-world objects as remembrance: Debbie used a first aid kit, for example, to help students remember that glial cells "fix" neurons (see page 48).

Repeated retellings: As students read, they stop at selected spots in the text and draw something or write a word that will help them remember what that section is about. At each stop, students return to the first stopping point and retell what that section was about, based on their word or picture and then continue with the retelling until they reach the latest stopping point.

Role play: Students take on the roles of various characters and dramatize the scene (see page 101).

Roll call review: Students respond to the roll call by saying one thing they remember from the previous lesson or from the readings.

Running review: Keep an ongoing list of topics and/or stories that have been studied in a prominent place in the classroom. Then periodically go through the list with students, recalling the most important points of each topic or story.

Save the last word for me: A discussion technique in which each participant brings a quotation from the reading and a written response to that quotation. The conversation starts with someone reading the quotation. Everyone shares his or her thoughts about the quotation. The conversation ends when the person reads his or her own original response to the quotation.

Secret reading assignment: Everyone reads the same assignment but marks the important passages based on a "secret" reading assignment.

Sketch-to-Stretch: At the end of a story, students respond to the prompt, "Draw what the story means to you." The purpose is to elicit the theme of the story, rather than a literal retelling.

Sorts: Students sort a list of words, often on individual cards, into categories. In a closed sort, the teacher provides the categories (e.g., words that change the _–y_ to _–i_ before adding _–es_ and those that don't). In an open sort, students determine the categories.

Sticky notes to record questions, etc.: Students can code a text, respond to a question, add information, and so on, by writing and posting sticky notes.

Storytelling hand: A hand can be a quick reminder of the key parts of a story: thumb = characters, index finger = setting, middle finger = problem, ring finger = events, pinkie = ending. Some teachers then trace a heart on the palm and ask for the theme of the story.

Think/pair/share: Pose a question and set aside quiet time for students to consider it on their own. Then have them get with a partner and share their ideas.

Thinking time: After asking a question, count to 5 or 7 or 10 before calling on a student to respond.

Thumbnail sketches: Students draw quick sketches roughly the size of a postage stamp to get an idea across quickly.

Timelines: Students often struggle to understand the relationships between events in history. A timeline can help them visualize when an event happened and what else was happening in the world at the same time.

Tree Map: A David Hyerle thinking map that identifies the components of an idea (as opposed to the brace map's focus on the components of a physical object).

Two-column note: One popular format is quotation and response; another is important information to list and interesting details.

Two pluses and a wish: A quick way to get a sense of your students' response to a presentation by you or a fellow student is to have them write two pluses and a wish to share with you or the student.

Two-word strategy: After students read a passage, ask them to think of two words that will help them remember the passage's content. Then they share their two words and rationale with other students as a review.

Using simpler examples: One strategy for figuring out how to solve a difficult math problem is to solve a similar but simpler problem. We use the same concept in helping students in their writing or in understanding a character's motivation.

Venn diagrams: These are the traditional way to show comparison/contrast. David Hyerle uses a "double-bubble" format that allows for a clearer comparison with more room to write.

Vote with your feet: The teacher puts quotations reflecting differing perspectives on a specific issue or subject on cards throughout the room. Then students move to the cards that most closely correspond to their beliefs. As students get more information, they can "vote with their feet" to change their responses.

Word predictions based on skimming: Readers skim the material to get the gist of the content and context for new vocabulary words.

Quick and Easy Reading Assessments

1. Cloze Assessment

A cloze assessment is a quick and easy way to check on a student's ability to read a text using meaning and syntax, and it can be constructed from any text being used in the classroom. Simply select a passage of about 100 words from a text you are using with your students. Copy the passage, leaving a blank for every seventh word. Make sure that each blank is equal in length, so students won't be guessing the missing word by how long or short it is. Ask students to insert the missing words as they read the passage out loud. To score, count up the number of words the students inserted that were either the actual word from the original text or a synonym and the correct part of speech for that word. Determine the percentage of correctly identified words. A score of 90% or better is an independent level, 60%–89% is an instructional level, and 59% or below is called the frustration level.

Example: The following is a 104-word passage from the Newbridge-published supplemental science text *Wind Power* by David Neufeld, set up as a cloze assessment.

> A wind turbine looks like a (gigantic) fan. But a wind turbine does (not) work like a fan. It works (in) reverse. Instead of using electricity to (make) wind, a wind turbine uses the(wind) to make electricity. Wind turbines transform (the) wind's energy into electricity that lights (buildings), runs computers, and provides the power (for) thousands of other tasks.
>
> All wind (turbines) have a few basic parts. The (three-bladed) rotor faces the wind. The (wind) turns the rotor blades, spinning a (shaft) that is connected to a generator. (The) generator makes electricity. The faster the (shaft) turns, the more energy is made.

A fourth-grade student read this passage, inserting the words as follows:

> A wind turbine looks like a regular fan. But a wind turbine does not work like a fan. It works in reverse. Instead of using electricity to make wind, a wind turbine uses the wind to make electricity. Wind turbines transform the wind's energy into electricity that lights houses , runs computers, and provides the power for thousands of other tasks.
>
> All wind turbines have a few basic parts. The turbine rotor faces the wind. The wind turns the rotor blades, spinning a blade that is connected to a generator. Turbine generator makes electricity. The faster the rotor turns, the more energy is made.

The shaded responses are those that are incorrect. This student inserted 9 of the 14 words correctly, considering that *houses* is an acceptable substitution for *buildings*. This is a score of 64%. Based on the scoring guide described above, *Wind Power,* a Level S text, is an instructional text for this student.

2. Running Record

A second quick and easy assessment is a running record of a passage of 100–120 words. This passage can be taken from any text that you are using with students for guided practice. Ask students to read the passage while you code their reading on a running record form (see pages 162–163). For most students in grades three and above, coding just the student errors is sufficient. Note substitutions, insertions, deletions, multiple attempts at words, and words for which students appeal for help. Also observe how fluent the reading is (i.e., whether the student reads with phrasing and expression and attends to punctuation).

When the student has finished reading the passage, ask him or her to retell what he or she has read. Use the appropriate fiction or nonfiction scoring guide on the provided running record form. Also, ask two deeper-level comprehension questions that draw on the student's ability to visualize and make connections while reading. Use the guide on the running record form to score the student's responses.

Tally each of the student's errors and self-corrections. (See the sample running record on pages 160–161.) Then score the running record by determining the following:

- **The error rate:** Divide the number of words read by the number of errors. This can be expressed as a ratio (e.g., 1:8 means the student made one error for every eight words read).

- **The accuracy rate:** Divide the number of errors made by the number of words read and express that figure as a decimal. Multiply this by 100 and subtract the sum from 100 to determine the percentage of words read accurately.

- **The self-correction rate:** Add the number of errors and self-corrections and divide this sum by the number of self-corrections. Express this figure as a ratio (e.g., 1:3 means one out of three errors was self-corrected).

For each error, analyze which cue(s) the student used—meaning, language structure or syntax, or visual aspects of the word—to make those errors. For each self-correction, analyze which cues the student used to make both the error and the self-correction. Review this analysis to see how the student is processing text. Ask yourself: Is the student self-monitoring? Does the student cross-check one cue system against another to figure out words? When the student is stuck, does he or she search for more information to solve the word? Is the student using all the information available in the text—meaning, syntax, and visual—to solve challenging words? Does the student self-correct?

Summarize your observations in the section provided on the running record form.

Finally, on the running record form, document the error, accuracy, and self-correction rates; check off the reading level, record the level of fluency, and make any other notes/observations about the student's reading. Use all this information to choose appropriate texts for your students and to inform your instruction.

For teachers who are not familiar with running records—coding, scoring, and analyzing—resources are available. Two notable resources are the CD-based *Sensitive Observation of Reading Behavior,* produced by the Reading Recovery Council of North America and *Running Records: A Self-Tutoring Guide* by Peter H. Johnston, published by Stenhouse Publishers.

Running Record/Follow-up Check

Name: _Amber_   Date: _2/2010_   **Reading Level**
- ☐ Independent 97-100%
- ☒ Instructional 90-96%
- ☐ Frustration below 90%

Teacher: _Mrs. S_   Grade: _4_

Title: _Wind Power_   Level: _S_

# of words: _104_   Error Rate 1: _26_   Accuracy Rate _96_ %   Self-Correction Rate 1: _2_

# of errors: _4_

Fluency:
- ☐ Fluent, expressive, with phrasing, like everyday speech
- ☒ Minimal expression, short phrases, awkward pauses
- ☐ Little/no expression choppy, word/word

Retelling: Fiction

	Complete	Adequate	Limited
Characters	☐	☐	☐
Setting	☐	☐	☐
Problem	☐	☐	☐
Events	☐	☐	☐
Solution	☐	☐	☐

Retelling: Non-Fiction

	Complete	Adequate	Limited
Who?	☐	☒	☐
What?	☐	☒	☐
When?	☒	☐	☐
Where?	☐	☐	☒
Why?	☐	☒	☐

Key Comprehension Questions:

	Clear, relevant response	Somewhat clear and/or relevant response	Unclear, irrelevant response
1. What did you picture in your mind as you read this passage?	☒	☐	☐
2. What connections did you make to what you read in this passage?	☐	☐	☒ no resp.

Processing of text: Tends to rely on V cues initially, looking at chunks of words. At times cross-checks w/ M. Does SC using M, S, V - esp. S

Cues Used
M = meaning
S = structure
V = visual

Page		E	SC	E MSV	SC MSV
27	re- |rev·erse|SC reverse|	1		m s Ⓥ	ⓂⓈV
	electrically electricity	1		Ⓜ s Ⓥ	
	tra- |trans-|SC transform|	1		m s Ⓥ	mⓈⓋ

Page		E	SC	Cues Used M= meaning S = structure V = visual	
				E MSV	SC MSV
	building⋅ | sc buildings |		1	(MS)V	(MS)V
	provide provides		1	(MS)V	
	baskit | sc ✓ basic | parts R		1	MS(V) (MS)V	
	blăd-ed bladed		1	MS(V)	
	rotator rotor		1	(MS)V	
	sh— | ✓ shaft |			M S V 4 0 8	M S V 24 2

Running Record/Follow-up Check

NAME: _____   DATE: _____

TEACHER: _____   GRADE: _____

TITLE: _____   LEVEL: _____

READING LEVEL
- ☐ INDEPENDENT 97–100%
- ☐ INSTRUCTIONAL 90–96%
- ☐ FRUSTRATION BELOW 90%

# of words: _____   Error Rate 1: _____   Accuracy Rate _____ %   Self-Correction Rate 1: _____
# of errors:

Fluency:
☐ Fluent, expressive, with phrasing, like everyday speech
☐ Minimal expression, short phrases, awkward pauses
☐ Little/no expression choppy, word/word

RETELLING: Fiction

	Complete	Adequate	Limited
Characters	☐	☐	☐
Setting	☐	☐	☐
Problem	☐	☐	☐
Events	☐	☐	☐
Solution	☐	☐	☐

RETELLING: Nonfiction

	Complete	Adequate	Limited
Who?	☐	☐	☐
What?	☐	☐	☐
When?	☐	☐	☐
Where?	☐	☐	☐
Why?	☐	☐	☐

KEY COMPREHENSION QUESTIONS:

	Clear, relevant response	Somewhat clear and/or relevant response	Unclear, irrelevant response or no response
1. What did you picture in your mind as you read this passage?	☐	☐	☐
2. What connections did you make to what you read in this passage?	☐	☐	☐

Processing of text

Cues Used
M = meaning
S = structure
V = visual

Page		E	SC	E MSV	SC MSV

Page		E	SC	E MSV	SC MSV

Cues Used

M = meaning
S = structure
V = visual

Effective Note Taking in Guided Reading

✔ Note unique thinking evident in a student's conversation.

✔ Note affective responses—highly engaged, off-task, strong emotions.

✔ Note fluency for some group members (as they read quietly to you or as they reread passages in support of answers).

✔ Note evidence of processing when listening to oral reading—taking words apart on the run, miscues that interfere with meaning, monitoring and self-correcting that takes place.

✔ Note evidence of strategic processing that enhances the reader's power. Note when they connect, make inferences about, question, analyze, or critique texts.

✔ Note language of strategic processing—when children say, *I connected . . .* or *I noticed* (see page 329 in *Guiding Readers and Writers*).

✔ Note when someone is participating well, is not participating, is participating in a surface manner or is just NOT getting it. Plan to do something to address problems immediately.

✔ Note how fast/slow students process a text (when they stay with you). Note order of eye movements—whether they pay attention to text features such as captions, graphs, etc.

✔ Note language of interaction—how well they listen to and expand upon other group members. This language can be taught—*I agree with . . .*

✔ Note the ability of the student to provide evidence for thinking when answering questions—spontaneously or prompted.

✔ Note the reader's organizational skills—sticky notes, notes, tabs, highlighting, margin notes, etc.

✔ Note the reader's (natural or prompted) ability to respond to texts—oral, written, artistic, more reading.

© Jeffery L. Williams, 2002

Questions to Assist in Planning for Guided Practice

Use this chart to help you plan for and reflect on teaching and learning across all components of a guided practice lesson.

LESSON COMPONENT	QUESTIONS
1. Choosing a text	Think about where this group of students is in their literacy development: — What genre would be appropriate for these students at this time? — What is students' background knowledge? — What skills and strategies do they have control of, some control of, little or no control of? — Which text would present opportunities for this group to build on what they know and have learned as readers? — Which text would stretch and extend the learning of this group? — What are my own interests and background knowledge: Is there something I have just read that I can share with students to personalize the lesson?
2. Determining a focus for instruction	Consider what this group of students has been working on: — Is there a skill or strategy that needs more work? — Are they ready to be introduced to a new skill or strategy?
3. Introducing the text	Based on your knowledge of these students, think about these questions: — How can they connect this book to their own experiences as well as their previous experience with texts? — What might be confusing in the text that I should address before reading? — What do they need to know about how this text is structured? — Is this genre familiar or new? — What do these students need to know in order to be able to read this genre successfully? — What can I bring from my own experiences to help them make sense of the text?

4. Reading the text	Students should read the text or a section of the text independently or with a partner within the group. You now have the opportunity to briefly listen in with two or three students individually to observe how they are handling the text and what new challenges they're encountering, and to provide prompts that support and extend each student's learning. This individual attention can be set up so that you spend time with every student across two or three meetings of the group.
5. Discussing and revisiting the text	Focusing on meaning, have students discuss the message of the text and respond personally: — What was the main idea and/or theme of the text? — What questions were answered? — What questions have not yet been answered? — What new questions have been raised? — What connections to their own experiences did they make as they read? To what they know about the world? To other texts they have read?
6. Teaching for strategies	Consider the focus for the guided practice lesson and the observations made during the reading of the text: — Over which strategies do all or most of the students show they have control? — What successful processing can the teacher highlight and praise? — What strategies do all or most of the students need additional help with? — What will help this group to read not only this text but other texts?
8. Word work	Based on observations made during reading: — Are these students developing sensitivity to words so that they notice new vocabulary or interesting uses of words? — What words do these students need help reading? — Are students using temporary pronunciations that are close approximations to the difficult words? — What is the next thing these students need to know about how to take words apart while reading for easier decoding? — What vocabulary was misunderstood? — Do they need help in using context to better understand the meaning of words? — Do these students need help in recognizing and using word families (cognates)?
9. Follow-up: Now what?	At the end of the lesson, pull it all together by asking students to talk about what they have learned: — What did you learn about reading today? — How will this help you as a reader? — How can you use what you've learned to day as you read on your own? Also, reflect on which invitations for extending the reading you can offer. (Check out the "Desert Island" strategies in the appendix on pages 153–157.)

Responding to Students Within the Zone of Proximal Development

If you are not sure what to say to a struggling student, the following charts provide prompts that guide students without doing the reading work for them.

Each of these charts includes:

- specific examples of students' responses as they encounter difficulty in text
- the language teachers can use to guide students in thinking about and solving these problems during guided practice
- ways to determine if guidance was helpful to students and possible next steps in instruction

The order of the charts—meaning, syntax or language structure, and graphophonics—presupposes the order of thinking for the teacher, not necessarily the order for instruction. The focus on meaning is paramount—we read to understand the author's message. Teachers help students achieve this goal by guiding them to think about what makes sense to them and to use their knowledge of the world, of English language structure, and of how letters and words work together. The teacher will need to utilize the prompts and responses from these three charts flexibly, according to observations of students and their interaction with the text. Indeed, in their teaching, teachers use the same strategies that students are learning to use in their reading. These include:

Self-monitoring: We listen to students as they read and talk about text and respond to them in ways that support and extend their thinking. We monitor our teaching and responses by asking ourselves the following questions: Did that help? Do I need to change the focus of my prompting? Do I need to increase or lower the level of support? Am I encouraging the students' independence?

Cross-checking: We observe students' reading behavior and think about what we know about students, asking ourselves: Am I helping students use what they know to learn something new? Is my teaching on the cutting edge of students' learning? Are my students moving toward independent application of what they have learned? Am I following each student's unique path toward the goal of proficient reading?

Searching: As students encounter difficulty or show that they are gaining more control of the strategies we're teaching them, we think about what we can say or do to foster learning: What prompt would best help the student get back on track? How much support should I give so that the student is as independent as possible? What should be the next focus? The next level of text?

Self-correcting: Just like our students, we teachers make errors, and we need to correct them. As reflective teachers, we think about how students respond to our teaching and evaluate our book choices, book introductions, prompting, areas of instructional focus, grouping practices, and extensions of text to ensure we are effectively meeting students' needs. Then we make changes accordingly.

Meaning: Guiding Students to Use the Cognitive Strategies for Comprehension

IF A STUDENT . . .	THEN THE TEACHER CAN . . .	HOW DO WE KNOW THAT IT WORKED? WHAT'S NEXT?
Reads without noticing when meaning breaks down or when he/she has made error that affects comprehension	Prompt for self-monitoring by saying: *Did that make sense?* or *Where did you get confused?* We all let our minds drift at times when we read. When this happens, we know we have to reread and reconnect with text. Students might need to be reminded to do this.	Student is self-monitoring if he/she stops, asks for help, rereads, or searches for information in text. Accept and celebrate any approximations toward understanding and effective processing of text. Next, encourage student to continue reading and thinking about message of text and making personal connections or responses.
Does not understand what is happening in a text and has no way to get back on track	Consider first if text is at an appropriate level for student. It may be best to drop a level or return to shared reading using this or another text to build student's background knowledge and vocabulary. With a chapter book, you could read the first few chapters together with discussion and modeling of thinking strategies. With nonfiction, it might be helpful to drop a level or two to give student the opportunity to easily read books to build background knowledge for more difficult text. Another option with nonfiction text is to read chapters or sections as a shared reading and identify main ideas on note-taking chart. This gives student a model of how to continue reading and understanding the text. You could also direct student to reread smaller sections and use a variety of prompts to help him/her re-engage with text. Possible prompts: • Reread this and think what the author is trying to say. • Reread this and think what new questions you have about it. • What word or words are tricking you here? • Reread this and then draw a picture to go with the text.	Student is back on track if he/she is making connections to text, even if these are tenuous. If student can connect what the author says to own experiences or to other texts he/she reads, celebrate these efforts and encourage student to continue to respond personally to text, ask questions, and respond to it through writing, art, or discussion. If student can identify words that he/she cannot read and/or does not understand, spend time assisting student to decode these words or distinguish their meanings. Encourage use of temporary pronunciations to hold an unknown word in mind while inferring its meaning. In a later lesson, show student how and when to move from temporary pronunciations to a search for conventional ones.

IF A STUDENT . . .	THEN THE TEACHER CAN . . .	HOW DO WE KNOW THAT IT WORKED? WHAT'S NEXT?
Cannot make or confirm predictions about a story or nonfiction text	For fiction, help student notice cues in book title, chapter titles, pictures, blurbs at the back of the book, or on the inside flap. For nonfiction, direct students to title, table of contents, glossary, index, bold type, picture captions, and other features that help readers determine what a book is about.	For fiction, student is able to make/write predictions about what he/she thinks will happen in story and to confirm or modify these while reading. For nonfiction, student can contribute to a KWL (what I Know, Want to learn, and Learned from this book) or respond to an anticipation guide prior to reading. Student can add to the L portion of the KWL chart.
Cannot keep track of characters in story	Work with student to create character charts or maps on chart paper or bookmarks listing characters and their traits and behaviors. Model how to make inferences about characters from descriptions in text, what they do, and what they say.	Student uses charts to identify and distinguish characters in story and to better understand how they behave and interact with other characters. Next, student can create character maps to specifically describe selected characters or write a personal response about a character.
Has difficulty understanding elements of story (setting, characters, plot, etc.) and how these affect what happens	Assist student in visualizing setting and making inferences about what author says that describes and distinguishes setting, characters, and plot. Discuss ways in which these elements affect what happens.	Student can complete story map or respond to elements of "Storytelling Hand," i.e., identify characters, setting, problem, events, and solution on a separate finger on one hand (see page 156) Using background knowledge, students make predictions about what would happen if each elements was different.
Gets confused when setting changes	Reread together the section of text where setting changes and identify words or techniques author uses to signal a change of time or place. Ask student to share what he/she knows what connections he/she made, and how he/she visualized the setting. Discuss what is going on with character(s) or story line as these setting changes appear.	Student begins to understand what setting is and can determine if and how it affects story. Next, student can read more complicated text, where setting and changes in setting impact the plot, such as in *Under the Blood Red Sun* by Graham Salisbury.
Loses track of who is talking when there is a lot of dialogue in text	You may need to conduct a lesson through shared reading to model how student can identify speaker in a text. Encourage the student to use prior knowledge of character (see above) and visualize scenes in which dialogue takes place. You could use dialogue directly from text for a brief Readers Theater, assigning character roles to students to demonstrate use of dialogue in a text.	Student can add to his/her knowledge about characters from what they say and is able to make connections between characters and plot of story. Next, student can go on to read texts that have more complex character development and dialogue.

Appendix

IF A STUDENT . . .	THEN THE TEACHER CAN . . .	HOW DO WE KNOW THAT IT WORKED? WHAT'S NEXT?
Has difficulty gathering information from text	For nonfiction, assist student in determining text structure: compare/contrast, cause/ effect, or sequence. Using a graphic organizer that reflects structure, have student fill in information from text. Student can identify text features, i.e., charts, maps, graphs, diagrams, pictures with captions, bold words, glossary, etc., and information provided that supports understanding of topic. This information can be added to graphic organizer. For fiction, have student reread to identify key words to answer literal questions about text and create and answer literal questions using key words like *who, what, when, where, how.*	Student can choose and complete an appropriate graphic organizer to summarize story or information in nonfiction text. He/she can then use notes across texts related to a topic and synthesize this information, e.g., in report form. For fiction, student can successfully complete story map including characters, setting, problem, events, and solution.
Struggles to summarize a story	Use story maps to identify important parts of story. Ask: *What was this story/chapter mostly about? What in this chapter keeps the story moving?* Or, if necessary, model your own thinking about what is important. Use Kylene Beers' frame: "Somebody Wanted But So" to model giving a story summary.	Student can provide a quick summary of a simple text using a framing device, e.g., Kylene Beers' "Somebody Wanted But So" (see pp. 144–149) or storytelling hand. Next step would be to move to more complex narrative structures and practice summarizing.
Cannot determine what is important in text from what may be interesting but less important	Have student list information to remember that it relates to headings and subheadings and evaluate what is important that relates to them. Give a limited amount of time, e.g., a one-minute "radio broadcast," for student to relate to others the most important information learned from reading this text, thus compelling him/her to select more significant information.	Student can complete graphic organizer reflecting headings and subheadings in text and evaluate whether or not this information speaks to focus of these headings.

Planning & Managing Effective Reading Instruction Across the Content Areas

IF A STUDENT . . .	THEN THE TEACHER CAN . . .	HOW DO WE KNOW THAT IT WORKED? WHAT'S NEXT?
Cannot form an opinion or draw conclusions about a text or provide evidence to support an opinion or conclusion.	Break the text into sections to make thinking and critiquing more manageable for student. Ask student to reread sections of text with specific purpose of determining what he/she agreed/disagreed with, liked/disliked. In fiction, ask student to identify a character he/she liked/disliked and to go back into text to find key words, phrases, descriptions, or events that supported this opinion. In nonfiction, use a KWL chart for student to add to or modify his/her understanding of subject.	Student can reread effectively, locating and noting information, and understands that rereading is a way to read same text with a different purpose. Student is able to read and critique more difficult text comparing and reflecting on his/her own opinion versus those of the author.
Has difficulty determining point of view in a story	May need to teach point of view, comparing and contrasting first person, third person, and omniscient. Discuss why the author chose a particular point of view.	Student can identify point of view in story and its effect. Next, he/she can relate how a story would be different if told from another point of view.
Has difficulty when point of view changes within story	Reread together the section where point of view changes. Identify key words that signal a change in viewpoint. An anchor chart lists different points of view in story and character or characters used.	Student is able to note key words that signal a change in point of view and understand how that affects story. Next, students can read books with multiple points of view, such as *The Wanderer* by Sharon Creech.

Syntax: Guiding Students to Use Their Knowledge of the English Language

IF A STUDENT . . .	THEN THE TEACHER CAN . . .	HOW DO WE KNOW THAT IT WORKED? WHAT'S NEXT?
Runs through punctuation	Model how to read passage with phrasing and expression and encourage student to do the same.	Student rereads passage you modeled, using phrasing and expression.
Ignores commas	Discuss use of commas in text and how they affect comprehension. Model how to read passage attending to commas.	Student rereads the passage attending to and using commas appropriately.
Self-corrects at point of error but loses the meaning of sentence or passage or loses expression after self-correction	Ask: *Did that make sense? Think about the story and reread, making sure it makes sense to you.*	Student rereads independently with phrasing and expression.
Reads in a sing-song voice	Model reading passage with appropriate phrasing and expression	Student drops sing-song reading and rereads passage with phrasing and expression.
Overemphasizes syntax	Say: *Did that make sense? Reread that and think about the story.*	Student rereads with appropriate phrasing and expression demonstrating understanding
Is not reading in phrases	Using a mask with a phrase window (approximately ¾" x 3") or two small cards, show sentence to student one phrase at a time and say: *Read all that you see in the window.* Then have student reread sentence, without mask. It may be appropriate to discuss meaning and how reading in phrases helps to clarify author's message.	Student rereads sentence with appropriate phrasing and demonstrates comprehension. Phrasing begins to take precedence over speed.
Reads with flat expression	Model fluent reading of passage or section of text, emphasizing expression that denotes meaning.	Student rereads with better expression and demonstrates comprehension.
Gets lost in longer sentences	Use a mask to show one or two phrases at a time and ask student to read phrases shown, eventually reading entire sentence. Ask: *Does that make sense?* or write sentence on a strip and cut it up in phrases. Ask student to read it all as it's divided.	Student rereads with phrasing and expression that demonstrates comprehension. Phrasing takes precedence over speed.
Doesn't adjust rate appropriately for type of text	Discuss and demonstrate different rates of reading for various types of text—skimming, scanning, reading for pleasure, reading for information. Discuss difference in pace between an action-packed adventure story versus a reflective drama .	Student adjusts rate according to type of text. Pace of reading might need to be discussed as new types of text are introduced.

Graphophonics: Guiding Students to Use Their Knowledge of How Letters and Words Work

The charts below, based on the work of Fountas and Pinnell (2001), provide examples of problems students may have with words in intermediate and middle school texts. The prompts from the first chart help students notice and correct errors. The prompts in the second chart guide students to analyze tricky words. The language of the prompts is specifically composed to maximize the *student's* thinking and problem solving. It's actually best to begin by saying nothing and giving the student the opportunity to problem solve independently. If the student is stuck and stops, proceed by prompting with a low level of support initially— perhaps saying in an encouraging tone, "Try it!" When the student can't proceed without help, prompt him or her to look at the information he or she consistently ignores: meaning, syntax, or graphophonics.

Too much time away from attending to text will jeopardize the student's understanding of it. We teachers walk a fine line when guiding a student's reading and regularly have to make on-the-spot decisions about what is the best thing to do. It takes practice!

Guiding Students to Notice and Correct Errors

IF A STUDENT . . .	THEN THE TEACHER CAN . . .	HOW DO WE KNOW THAT IT WORKED? WHAT'S NEXT?
Stops at point of difficulty but doesn't make any attempt to problem solve	Ask: *Why did you stop?* or *What did you notice?* Encourage him/her by saying, *What could you try?*	Student makes an attempt to solve word. If he/she needs more support and guidance, use one of prompts listed in the section on word analysis on page 175.
Stops at a tricky word, then substitutes a non-sense word or other word	Say: *You knew that was a tricky word, and I like the way you tried something, but does that make sense?* It is helpful to read back to student entire sentence with substituted word and then ask if it makes sense.	Student rereads and corrects error. Allow him/her to continue reading without interruption. Possibly return to this after student reads selection, offering praise. Say: *I like the way you reread that and fixed it so it made sense to you* or—to encourage student to reflect on reading—say: *How did you know it was __?*
Substitutes a word that makes sense but does not match the word in text	Say: *That makes sense but does it look right?*	Student rereads and looks through word and/or takes it apart to correct error. Again, allow student to continue reading but possibly return to this as an example of effective problem solving.
Substitutes word or words that fit language structure of text but does not match actual word	Say: *That sounds right but does it look right?*	Student rereads and looks through word and/or takes it apart to correct error. Again, allow student to continue reading but possibly return to this as an example of effective problem solving.

IF A STUDENT . . .	THEN THE TEACHER CAN . . .	HOW DO WE KNOW THAT IT WORKED? WHAT'S NEXT?
Substitutes word that starts like word in the text	Say: *It starts like that. Now check the last part.*	Student looks through word and/or takes it apart to correct error. If student cannot solve word, continue with prompts listed in the section on analyzing words on page 175.
Substitutes word that starts and ends like word in text	Think about what student can do to problem solve word and then offer an appropriate prompt. Some prompts, ordered from low to high support, are: *Were you right? What's wrong? What's the tricky part of the word? You've got the first and last part of the word right. See if you can find out what's wrong.* *Check the middle part of the word.*	Student looks through word and/or takes it apart to correct error. If student cannot solve word, continue with prompts listed in section on analyzing words on page 175.
Gets bogged down in making multiple attempts at word that looks right or contains many of letters in word in text but does not fit meaning and/or language structure, e.g. says *word* for *world*	Encourage student to reread sentence or paragraph and think about meaning and/or language structure. Say: *Try that again and think what would make sense* or *Try that again and think what would sound right.*	Student rereads and successfully corrects error. If he/she cannot solve word, use prompts on page 175 to guide student to take it apart and/or make analogies to known words to successfully solve it.
Substitutes word that makes sense but is not word in text	**First,** consider if error is critical to understanding text. If it is not, ignore it. If it is, say: *That makes sense but does it look right?*	When student substitutes a word that preserves the meaning, this is an indication that he/she is reading for meaning. Thus, most of the time it's best to allow student to continue reading and return to word afterward to praise student's response, discuss word in question, and possibly spend time to analyze it using instructional techniques suggested on page 175 .
Substitutes word that sounds right but is not word in text	**First,** consider if error is critical to understanding text. If it is not, ignore it. If it is, say: *That sounds right but does it look right?*	Student rereads and successfully corrects error. If he/she cannot solve word, use prompts on page 175 to guide student to take it apart and/or make analogies to known words to successfully solve it.

Guiding Students to Analyze Words

IF A STUDENT . . .	THEN THE TEACHER CAN . . .	HOW DO I KNOW IT WORKED? WHAT'S NEXT?
Reads up to word and stops or substitutes nonsense word	Say: *Try that again and say the first part (chunk) of the word.*	Student rereads sentence or group of sentences, sounding first syllable or chunk of word, and reads word accurately. Student should continue reading uninterrupted. If this particular word is critical to meaning of text, return to it after reading to use context to clarify its meaning.
Encounters word and stops or substitutes another word for it	Say: *Do you know a word like that?* or *Do you know a word that starts like that? Ends like that?*	Student takes a second look at word and makes an attempt to solve it. If student is successful, encourage him/her to continue reading. If student cannot solve word, point out its known parts; for example, a prefix or suffix. Or write on a whiteboard known words that are analogous to word, e.g., *back* has same phonogram as part of word *shackled*. Whenever student spends time solving a word, direct him/her to reread sentence or group of sentences, now reading accurately word that caused the problem.
Encounters multisyllable word and stops or substitutes another word for it	Prompt student to take word apart to solve it using one or more of following prompts, ordered from low to high support: *Do you see a part that might help? Is that word like another word you know? Look for a part you know. Look at the first syllable. Notice the syllables. Look at the root word. Look at the prefix/suffix. Look at the ending of the word. Cover the last part of the word. Cover the first part of the word.*	As above, if student successfully solves word on own, have him/her continue reading. If student continues to have difficulty, provide more support to help him/her analyze word as suggested in section below, use context to discern its meaning, and reread sentence.
Substitutes word and stops or substitutes word or nonsense word that causes understanding to break down	Say: *Read that again and think of what the word could mean.*	Student rereads sentence accurately. If he/she is successful, continue reading. If student continues to have difficulty, use some of prompts in sections above, emphasizing that it needs to make sense.